Great Houses
of the Western World

Text by Nigel Nicolson
Photography by Ian Graham

Spring Books

London·New York·Sydney·Toronto

Original edition published 1968 and
© Copyright 1968 by George Weidenfeld & Nicolson
Ltd, London
Designed by Behram Kapadia to the pattern devised
by Pierre Faucheux for Hachette-Réalités

This edition published 1972 by
The Hamlyn Publishing Group Limited
London · New York · Sydney · Toronto
Hamlyn House, Feltham, Middlesex, England

Printed in Italy by
Arnoldo Mondadori Editore Officine Grafiche, Verona

ISBN 0 600 33885 1

Contents

Foreword

The entrance hall at Villa Agnelli, looking towards the fountain which veils the front façade. In the interior are examples of the simple Piedmontese stucco which is also found on the walls of the stairwell. Immediately on crossing its threshold, one finds oneself in a pleasantly well-lit house, decorated in the colours of a wedding-cake – white on white, pink on white, lemon on pale blue, and other variations.

The American houses described in this book were visited by the author in the autumn of 1966 and by Ian Graham a few months later. We also went separately to the houses in Great Britain. But we visited together all the houses on the mainland of Europe during the spring and summer of 1967. The percipient reader may be able to plot the progress of our four-months' journey from Rome to Stockholm by the slight seasonal changes detectable in the outdoor photographs. The description of each house was written either in the house itself as it was being photographed, or immediately after our visit to it. Everywhere we received from the owners or occupants a welcome and assistance without which we could not have completed our tasks so enjoyably, if at all. We also wish to thank Miss Katherine Macdonald, a young American, who accompanied us as secretary throughout most of Europe.

The houses were not chosen haphazard, nor left to chance encounters on the road, although two or three selected houses were dropped in favour of more attractive alternatives which we found in the neighbourhood. The first house in the book, Hochosterwitz in Austria, was one such discovery, and so were both houses in Czechoslovakia. In general I chose houses which are representative of different periods of their country's culture, which are in good (but, like Château d'Oiron, not always perfect) condition, and which were not too much altered by subsequent rebuilding. I have tried to keep a balance between different types of house, varying the size from the modest manor-house of Gunterstein in Holland to the imitation of Versailles which King Ludwig raised on a lake-isle in Bavaria; and the style from the lovely tower-house of Castle Fraser in Scotland to Jefferson's Monticello in Virginia. My original hope had been to choose only inhabited houses, but this proved too exclusive in the altered political conditions of Eastern Europe; and even in the United States only one out of five houses, Beauregard, is privately occupied.

The book, therefore, is an architectural anthology, not a guide to homes. It illustrates how Europeans changed their manner of building through some six hundred years, how each country acquired an individual style and influenced the style of others, and how the Continent as a whole gave something of permanent architectural value to America. It traces the development of sophisticated housing through thirty-six examples of the best.

It attempts to describe not only how men built, but how they lived in what they built. A great house was not simply an elegant façade, rising like a curtain on two or three set scenes within. It was also a boxing-together of domestic conveniences, and the hub of many other lives than those of the family which owned it. There was probably a garden around it, and an estate beyond. There were attic rooms and outhouses which the owner might not enter for years, but which were as important for the running of his house as the drawing-room was to his self-esteem. Now that the majority of the great houses are no longer occupied on the scale for which they were designed, we tend to look upon them, and to display them, as parade-rooms for aristocratic finery instead of places where people ate, dozed, bathed, cooked, died, gave birth and awoke screaming in the night. In imagination we must supply the smells, sights and sounds which were contemporary with the building and have now been replaced by others. How easy it is, for example, to forget the importance of horses in every age depicted in this book; or the difficulty of producing light and water when and where required; or the absence of proper drains and even of corridors – for cleanliness and privacy, which one would suppose to be among the earliest civilised needs of man, were among the last to be satisfied by architects.

Six of the houses are not regularly or periodically open to the public. They are: Castle Fraser, Gunterstein, the Villa Agnelli, Schönborn and both houses in Denmark. The others can be seen, by or without a previous appointment. Many of them attract hundreds of thousands of visitors a year. The freedom from human clutter noticeable in some of Ian Graham's photographs does not indicate that the houses were neglected by tourists when we were there, but that he was patient or the guides were kind. The popularity of these houses, from Sarospatak on the eastern border of Hungary to Stratford, Virginia, increases annually. What do the people come to see? A general's walking-stick or a Savonnerie carpet? Both. There is an insatiable human interest in how other humans live or have lived. The proof of it is that the interior of a house always seems to appeal more than its exterior, even if the latter be much finer. 'May we go inside?' is a request which would please every architect if not every owner, for it is one of the aims of architecture to arouse curiosity in what lies behind. This book goes inside.

Sissinghurst Castle, Kent, England   N.N.

A side-door at Schloss Schönborn, near Vienna, which was built in the early 18th century to the designs of the great Austrian architect, Lukas von Hildebrandt. The character of this baroque house is one of classical restraint enlivened by that sudden fieriness of stone ornament by which all Hildebrandt's work was distinguished.

9

Hochosterwitz *Carinthia Austria 1570-86*

The castle explodes out of the Austrian countryside. In this land of spectacular scenery, it is a phenomenon. Even bare of buildings the rock would seem like a castle, so precipitous is the cliff-face and so abrupt its pinnacles, and the skirt of pine-forest which covers the lower slopes accentuates the remoteness of the summit. Were there but one building on the top, everyone would wish to know its history. But the view from the plain below takes in a whole group of buildings, including a church with steeple and a chain of towers looped around the mountain until the last disappears into the trees. The explanation is not hard to guess. This is a position of natural strength fortified to the point of inaccessibility by a family of great determination and resources. The uppermost works form the dwelling-house and garrison's quarters; the chain of towers guards the approach-way. These are the hard facts: Hochosterwitz was built between 1570 and 1586 by Baron George Khevenhüller, Governor of Carinthia, as a main bastion of defence against the Turkish invaders. It has remained almost unaltered from that day to this.

It is a fortress, but it is also a work of architecture, which justifies its position at the beginning of this book. To what degree any thoughts beyond purely military needs entered the mind of the Italian engineer, Domenico dell' Aglio, who probably planned it, can only be imagined. But there are touches of decoration (a pair of unnecessary pilasters here, a nicely calculated roof-line there) which suggest that Khevenhüller was not in the least indifferent to the aesthetic, and even romantic, impact which his castle would make upon the chance traveller. We find representations of it in etchings and in the background of paintings from the early 17th century onwards, conveying something of the startled delight which the first sight of the place induced then and still induces. And not only the first sight; for as you wander around its base, treading on pine-needles or through high corn, it reveals a constantly changing silhouette, and the rising or sinking sun (and the rising or sinking moon) will light up different facets of its many buildings, separating them from each other and giving the whole composition a freshness, a piquancy and a variety which are never sated by familiarity.

OPPOSITE *The castle from the south-west, which is the side turned away from the lowest entrance gates. The full display of approach-towers is illustrated by the print which was made by J. W. Valvasor in 1688. The print slightly exaggerates the drama of the approach and the cragginess of the hill, but in essentials it is accurate. The castle proper is concentrated on the summit, with the church just below it: all the other towers are placed at intervals along the road which is festooned round the conical hill.*

OPPOSITE *The castle church from one of the upper windows, and the plain of Carinthia beyond. The roof of the church has its original shingle tiles, like scales, but the turret to the right is re-covered in wooden slats, like the sloping wall-top in the foreground.* ABOVE *One of the smaller approach-towers through which the road passes on its way to the summit, with the church above and two flanking turrets covering the steep and winding ascent.*

From among the buildings themselves there are constant surprise views, both upwards and downwards. The long ascent holds something in reserve until the very top, like a pilgrimage, and the changing spatial relationship of tower to tower, blank wall to needle-pointed steeple, produces a sense of exhilaration, of mounting achievement, that eases the labour of the climb. Between the embrasures of the battlements or through gun-ports, you catch glimpses of the countryside which you left far below. The view from Hochosterwitz is as astonishing as the view of it. The pine-covered hills flow around it, keeping a respectful distance, and the cornfields sweep down the valleys to its base, leaving in their train scattered villages and the lovely Carinthian version of the church-spire which stands sentinel over the land more benignly even than the Norman towers of other countries. As you mount the pathway (a jeep could be, and has been, used, but Hochosterwitz demands the penance and tribute of the climb on foot), you draw level with the tree-tops and can then look down into them—triangular shadows stabbing downwards between pine-pyramids stabbing upwards. Further off, the edge of a wood is exposed by a sudden precipice, and the tall bare pine-trunks march up the slope like Grenadiers. Who can doubt that the weary defenders of the region drew consolation from this view of what they were defending?

In fact, Hochosterwitz was never attacked. The Turkish tide receded almost at the moment when the fortress was completed. But it played its part as a deterrent in discouraging any renewal of the invasion, and it affirmed the status of the Khevenhüller family. It was but one, though the greatest, of the many castles which they controlled in southern Austria, and they found it useful during the troubles that followed the religious controversies of the time, in which they took a leading part on the Protestant side. One can see proof of their double purpose – for God and the fatherland – above almost every gateway, for George Khevenhüller set a tablet inscribed in Latin on every one of his fourteen approach towers, proclaiming his piety and his patriotism, and the date when the tower was completed. Owing to the excellence of the original work and the fact that it was never destroyed by the enemy and barely altered by its later owners, we can trace the military purpose of the place exactly.

Few people could be so indifferent to fortifications as to ignore so dramatic and complete an example as this. It was built in an age of cannon ; therefore there must be no place where a sudden fierce bombardment followed by an assault could carry the fortress by surprise. The enemy must be obliged to claw his way up to the innermost defences tower by tower. Each tower was a self-contained fort: it was sited and provisioned to stand a separate siege. If a back-way were found to the top of the cliff-face – an impossibility, but it was guarded against – the enemy would then have to reduce a dozen subsidiary garrisons below. The defences, in other words, were spread-eagled across all the upper slopes of the mountain-cone, and it is this dispersion which makes the castle seem from below so much larger than it really is.

The one main approach was by a roadway some ten feet wide which passes in turn under each of the fourteen gateways, spaced fifty to a hundred yards apart. Each gives covering fire to its neighbour, above and below, and at intervals there are bastions for artillery or turrets for small-arms guarding the approach at long and short range from new directions. The roadway climbs steeply in a spiral round the cone, and near the top twice doubles back on itself, providing additional points of vantage for the defenders. As the modern visitor climbs this *via dolorosa* he comes one by one to the different barriers which he would have faced as an enemy. They are so formidable and so ingenious that it is only the recollection of the terrifying violence of the Turkish invasions that stifles one's amusement. This was no joke. Every tower, every loophole, was sited with extreme care to bring to bear the maximum volume of fire on the most threatened points. No two gateways are the same. One will have a portcullis which could be dropped unexpectedly from above; another will be guarded on each side by a drawbridge crossing deep crevices in the cliff; in a third the drawbridge is inside the tower, so that any attacker who managed to force its gates would be met by an impassable chasm where he least expected it, and, on the far side, contemplate the underside of the drawn-up bridge barring all further progress. Below on the right was the cliff ; above on the left was the cliff. This was only one of fourteen such barriers. Clearly the

TOP *The seventh tower on the way up is named after the builder of Hochosterwitz, George Khevenhüller, whose bust appears above the central opening, in full armour but without his helmet. The inscription records that the tower was built in 1580. Although it was primarily a military work, the effect of the Renaissance is seen in the two Tuscan pillars and the scroll-work around the inscription.* ABOVE *The tomb of George Khevenhüller, originally in the castle church but now removed to the upper rooms of the castle itself. The figure is of painted wood, dating from the late 16th century, and the altar is of gilded bronze.* OPPOSITE *'The view from Hochosterwitz is as astonishing as the view of it. The pine-covered hills flow around it, keeping a respectful distance, and the cornfields sweep down the valleys to its base, leaving in their train scattered villages and the lovely Carinthian version of the church-spire which stands sentinel over the land.' This view is from the gallery at nearly the highest point of the castle.*

place could only be reduced by starving it out. They had thought of this too: apart from underground storerooms, there were immense wells of clear water, and butts in every tower.

But again one turns from the military to the architectural merits of this astonishing place. The castle at the top is quite plain, incorporating a round tower and a simple little chapel dating from an earlier and less elaborate castle on the same site. Its walls enclose a courtyard, shaded by trees which barely grow level with the parapet walks, and a well-head which supports a miniature forest of seedlings on its moss-covered pents. The rooms around it are very simple, interesting internally only for the views from the windows and the battery of weapons which they contain. There are different forms of staging built up around the courtyard, like sets for a play, and this variety of level and outlook makes the summit of the castle as fascinating as its approach. In about 1670 an external gallery was added, ending in a curved iron-work balcony which casually fends the visitor from a precipitous drop. There is something Spanish about this corner – a cool white cloister and a balcony overlooking a stupendous view – but look to the right, and there is Austria again in the presence of the castle church, a delicate thing to perch so high, with its original roof of shell-shaped slate and its two barefooted penitents standing in stone each side of the door, carvings made in Italy but symbolic of the Governor's conversion to the new faith.

In a corner of the courtyard he left his longest and most admonitory Latin inscription. 'Under the protection of Almighty God', it begins, 'George Khevenhüller of Aichelberg, Freiherr of Landskron, heir to Hochosterwitz, Master of the Horse to the Emperors Ferdinand I, Maxmilian II and Rudolf II . . .' and so on, through all his titles, '. . . has raised this fortified house at his own expense but for the protection of the State. And he leaves instructions that it must never pass out of the hands of his family, whether by sale or mortgage or by dividing up the estate or by gift or dowry or any other means.' The tablet is dated 1576. Nearly four hundred years later the pledge is still binding. Hochosterwitz belongs today to Fürst Franz Khevenhüller-Metsch, the direct descendant of George Khevenhüller. It is a pleasant sight, after completing the arduous ascent, to find this seventy-year-old Prince walking round the uppermost courtyard of his castle, welcoming the people who come in thousands to enjoy the view, as once his ancestors patrolled the same parapets with very different intent.

ABOVE *On arrival at the top, one is surprised to find so rural and unmilitary a courtyard. The only reminder that this was the keep of one of the strongest fortresses in Central Europe are the water-butts below the far arches, which survive from the age of sieges. In addition, there were two deep wells within the upper compound of the castle.* BELOW *The castle is not now inhabited, but some rooms in the highest part have been fitted up by the present owner, Fürst Khevenhüller-Metsch, for occasional use. This small library in its timber grid is part of the suite.* OPPOSITE *Some of the 16th-century armour is still preserved in the castle, with a life-size effigy of the huge Captain of the Guard.*

Penshurst Place *Kent England 1340-1607*

It is only possible to describe this beautiful, puzzling house historically. For not only do the names of its many owners read like the *dramatis personae* of all Shakespeare's historical plays combined, but it grew slowly for three centuries, and then for three more was repaired, modernised, re-Gothicised and in part rebuilt. No owner was indifferent to what he found. He added to it or adapted it. In consequence there are few places in Britain more teasing to the archaeologist who attempts to date its various parts, and few where the ordinary visitor will find so much to illustrate how men built and lived (and therefore how they thought) throughout those six centuries.

The house is loosely knit. Almost every part of it is but one room thick. Wing was added to wing at different times, and brick was piled on earlier stone. Mediaeval towers were left isolated or incorporated in a Tudor structure. You need a ground-plan to find your way about the rooms and centuries. But Penshurst is only romantic to those who sentimentalise ancient disarray. It is tough and vigorous. Apart from the Long Gallery, there are no interiors which set out to charm. Yet it is a very seductive house. Because it is so spread-out, shaped roughly like the arms of a swastika, it is full of light. One wing closes the view from another, forming three-sided courtyards and skylines of chimneys, dormers, gables, towers and battlements. It looks outwards too. There is a park and a lovely walled garden, each, like the house, the product of slow maturity. Penshurst is still as Ben Jonson described it after a visit there in 1616, in one of the most elaborate bread-and-butter letters ever penned to a host and hostess :

'Thou art not, Penshurst, built to envious show,
   Of touch, or marble ; nor can boast a row
Of polished pillars, or a roofe of gold :
   Thou hast no lantherne, whereof tales are told ;
Or staire, or courts ; but stand'st an ancient pile,
   And these grudg'd at, art reverenc'd the while …
Now, Penshurst, they that will proportion thee
   With other edifices, when they see
Those proud, ambitious heaps, and nothing else,
   May say, their lords have built, but thy lord dwells.'

ABOVE *The mediaeval stairway rising from one end of the Baron's Hall to the Solar.* OPPOSITE *The King's Tower, begun by Sir Henry Sidney in the last year of his life, 1585-6, and finished by his son Robert, to replace the mediaeval entrance. The Elizabethan steward of Penshurst recorded that Sir Henry set the tower slightly askew, 'so that he might see clear through the porch and service corridor of the hall to the garden'. Hence the three archways in perspective, of which the most distant is that of the garden tower.*

One of the ten life-size figures supporting the chestnut roof of the Baron's Hall. They are lay figures of men and women who worked for Sir John Pulteney six hundred years ago.

OPPOSITE *The interior of Penshurst's mid 14th-century hall, which is the finest domestic hall left in Britain, and one of the very few which retains its central hearth (left), from which the smoke escaped through vents in the roof. The tall Gothic windows and the huge timber roof recall ecclesiastical buildings of the same period. 'It is a barn magnified, a nave secularised . . . The greater the space to be spanned, the higher the roof to span it, like a ship's hull in reverse.'*

One can confidently begin the story in 1340, not with documents or enigmatic foundations, but with a building still so complete, so striking, that in any other place everything that came after it would seem an anti-climax. The original 14th-century manor – or all of it that matters – stands at the centre of the present house. It consisted of porch, hall, undercroft, solar and servants' quarters. Perhaps there was also a chapel and an entrance gateway with an encircling wall, for it is unlikely that the porch led directly out of fields, but if so, these have gone, like the kitchen which lay outside the main hall-block, connected to it by a central passage. You still enter the house by the hall. There has been no other entrance to it from the court since the late 18th century, when the side-door was walled up. It makes a staggering first impression. It is very large, its roof spanning nearly forty feet at a single leap without internal columns, and it has remained unaltered since it was built soon after 1340 by Sir John Pulteney, a Mayor of London who purchased the manor in that year.

The hall could almost date from a century earlier, so little change had there been since wealthy men first began to build their halls at ground level instead of on the first floor of a keep. There is a low dais at one end – a six-inch step to separate master from servants – a gallery supported by a screen at the other, two fair-sized rooms beyond it above the larder and buttery, huge windows in each side-wall and high up in the gables, a timber roof, and a brick-tiled floor. That is all. It is indescribably empty. There was no fireplace, and none was added later. Instead, an octagonal hearth was laid with logs in the middle of the floor, and the smoke billowed up, free and blinding, to escape from the roof by a louvre. Several long tables, of which two, dating from about 1450, survive, were arranged lengthwise down the centre. It is a barn magnified, a nave secularised, for the daily assembly of the entire household in the hall was as traditional as the congregation of the whole village in the parish church, and the only known method of enclosing rooms large enough for both purposes was by building high: the greater the space to be spanned, the higher the roof to span it, like a ship's hull in reverse.

The result is a superb piece of architecture. Its obvious inconvenience makes it all the more remarkable that it has remained untouched for so long. One can only guess at the motives of later owners of Penshurst for saving it, for its survival is almost unique, and only in the last two hundred years have antiquarian interests prevailed over ridicule for such uncouth splendour. The hall, however, had its advantages. It could be used for great occasions in the summer; smaller, more serviceable, rooms were incorporated in its structure at either end; no doubt the storage space was found useful. So solidly was it built that the main hall required no major repairs until 1910, and it would have been almost as expensive to demolish it as to build it anew. In 1471 one reads in the accounts of payment to a man for catching hawks in the upper rafters, but there is no mention of structural defects. So it was allowed to stand intact. It formed a great central mass to which buildings could be added. It became a hub and perhaps a symbol: very gradually it became an object of wonder.

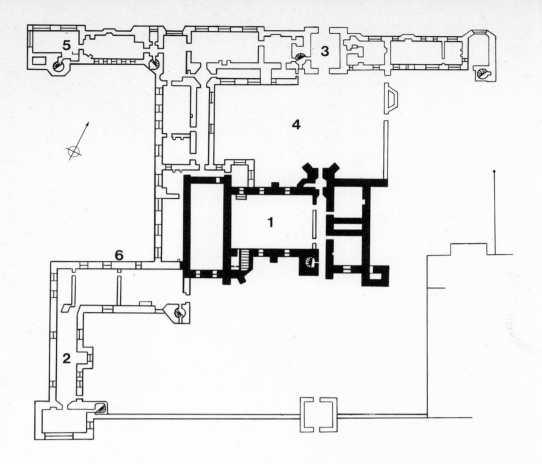

Penshurst is composed of a 14th-century core (shown in solid black) from which at different periods during the next 250 years wings were thrown out to link it with a ring of mediaeval towers, forming courts and half-courts. 1. Baron's Hall. 2. Long Gallery. 3. King's Tower. 4. Entrance Court. 5. President's Tower. 6. Buckingham Building.

One main stair rose out of the hall, at its south-west corner, a curving stone flight winding up an external tower with treads six feet long and so massive that you could still ride a horse up them. It led to the solar. This was a long room for the family with a central hooded fireplace and was probably unpartitioned. Clearly these two great rooms, the hall and solar, would no longer satisfy the new owners of Penshurst in the late 14th and early 15th centuries. They built an extension leading west from a corner of the solar, almost as large as the hall itself. For centuries it has been known as the Buckingham Building, after the Dukes of Buckingham who owned Penshurst from 1446 to 1521. But it must be earlier in date. One can attribute it either to Sir John Devereux (the owner from 1382 to 1393) or to the Duke of Bedford (1430-5) or to his brother, the Duke of Gloucester (1435-46), after whom it was called as late as 1607. It has been so much altered that it is now impossible to fix its date or exact purpose. We cannot tell how many floors it held, nor how exactly it was divided by partitions. Nor do we know what other buildings were added to the hall in later mediaeval times. Around the house there were five or six turrets which may have resulted from Devereux's licence to crenellate his house in 1392; and one reads in documents of the 'Great Stables' and the 'Great Tower', which suggest outbuildings which have disappeared. Certainly there must have been extensive accommodation by 1519, when the third Duke of Buckingham entertained King Henry VIII 'with great magnificence'. The design of the buildings forming the south-west corner of the main courtyard indicates that it may have been one of Buckingham's extensions. If so, the plan of Penshurst was beginning to emerge before the manor was given to the Sidneys by King Edward VI in 1552.

RIGHT *The Buckingham Building (6 on the plan) was the first extension to be added to the mediaeval manor. It was built at some period between 1380 and 1450, but its exact purpose and interior arrangements are uncertain. The three great windows, splaying inwards to admit more light, are original, but the three above are Elizabethan.* BELOW *The range of buildings seen from the south. From left to right are the big end-window of the long gallery, the Buckingham Building, the solar, the Baron's Hall with its turret staircase, and the garden tower.*

However great the names that have so far been paraded, it is always with the Sidneys that Penshurst will be associated. For one reason, they were the first owners to regard it as their home instead of a convenient and profitable Kentish annexe to other estates. For another, they still own it four hundred years later, in the person of William Sidney, Viscount De L'Isle. For a third, this family produced sons and daughters who played great roles in the State, and by their grace and courage aroused affection as well as admiration, generation after generation. Contemporaries regarded one of them, Sir Philip Sidney, the poet, courtier, statesman and soldier, as the man by whom they would wish the whole Elizabethan age to be remembered. When he died aged 32 of wounds received at the battle of Zutphen, Camden wrote of him : 'This is that Sidney who as Providence seems to have sent him into the world to give the present a specimen of the ancients, so it did on a sudden recall him and snatch him from us as more worthy of heaven than of earth.' Over two hundred years later Shelley, whose family was connected with the Sidneys, could write in his *Adonais* :

> 'Sidney, as he fought
> And as he fell, and as he loved and lived,
> Sublimely mild, a spirit without spot.'

A room is still pointed out at Penshurst as the room where this paragon was born, and he spent much of his boyhood there. But he owned it for no more than the five months between his father's death in May and his own in October, 1586, and he left no physical mark upon it. It was his father, Sir Henry Sidney, and his brother Robert who gave Penshurst its final form. All later changes were complementary. In the 19th century the cult of the antique coincided with loss of architectural self-confidence, and when later Sidneys restored or modified the house, they did so externally in the style which was contemporary with these two men. Internally they allowed themselves a little more licence in the Gothic tradition.

Sir Henry Sidney (1529-86) and his second son, Robert Sidney, later first Earl of Leicester (1563-1626), identified most of their work by tablets on outside walls, or by initials on rainwater-heads and on inside panelling. The sequence of their building or rebuilding is therefore fairly clear. It was probably in 1560-2, when the accounts record unusual activity by masons, carpenters and tile-makers, 'working on my lord's work', that Sir Henry threw out the northern wing, linking it southwards with the Buckingham Building and westwards with one of the mediaeval towers, which he widened and heightened. Along the ground floor he inserted an open colonnade of seven arches, and added an octagonal turret of brick, within which a beautiful oak staircase spirals up to the room where Sir Philip Sidney was, by tradition, born. Finally, in the last year of his life, 1585-6, he replaced the presumed mediaeval entrance by the King's Tower, which is still the main entrance from the park, setting it slightly askew, as his steward recorded, 'so that he might see clear through the porch and service corridor of the hall to the garden'.

ABOVE *The beautifully constructed staircase which mounts the octagonal brick turret to the different floors of the President's Tower, where Sir Philip Sidney is supposed to have been born in 1554.* OPPOSITE *The Long Gallery runs southwards at right-angles to the Buckingham Building and was completed in 1607. It is unusually airy, being lit by windows on both sides and at the far end, through which there are uninterrupted views over the park and garden.'It has a festive, summery quality . . . It is cool and light and demands to be filled with flowers.'*

The house was by this time virtually complete. Robert finished his father's entrance tower (the doors carry the initials of himself and his wife), built a new stable block, and after some delay completed the Long Gallery in 1607, a building which his father probably started. This room is without doubt the loveliest in the house. The Elizabethan-Jacobean formula was followed with subtle variations. It runs along the upper storey of the southern-most wing, with unencumbered views over the garden and the park, and widens at the end into a panelled chamber formed from the first floor of another of the mediaeval towers. The central bay opposite the fireplace gives the gallery additional variety. It thus avoids the cigar-box lines of many such galleries, affording privacy at different points down its great length. It has a festive, summery quality, it is a room for music or flirtation; it is cool and light and demands to be filled with flowers. Below it is a second gallery, which the present Lord De L'Isle has cleared of clutter to re-form a nether-gallery which leads to the garden.

Penshurst, indeed, is one vast garden-house. As early as the written records begin, we read of the care which was given to the terracing, pools and cultivation of fruit-trees. The letters exchanged between Robert Sidney and his wife and agents are full of references to new plantings. You can see the result of it today in the marriage between house and garden, for both are still beautifully maintained. But Penshurst is a marriage between centuries too. F. S. Boas, Sir Philip Sidney's latest biographer, has summed up his character as 'combining in himself some of the salient features of mediaevalism and of the Renaissance'. The same is true of his house. Its slim strong lines are the product of discipline and innovation, of clear intention and haphazard growth. Almost any one of its many façades reveals patchwork of a kind, so that the house as a whole can be read off like an architectural textbook. But with what skill and love was it assembled and extended, and its decaying parts restored! If it is ever legitimate to attribute to stone and brick and glass and timber a character which is the sum of all its past inhabitants, such a house is Penshurst. It is amusing to decipher its different periods, but the attempt must not be allowed to destroy the Arcadian quality of the whole. The search for information can render a house more intelligible but less understood. As Richard Church wrote of Penshurst, 'There is such a thing as too much longing for knowledge' of how it came to be what it is.

26

LEFT *The President's Court, a quarter of it brick, three-quarters of it stone, is formed by several buildings of different date with no attempt at achieving symmetry. It is still Gothic in feeling, but Sir Henry Sidney's colonnade of seven arches introduces a new note. They run towards the President's Tower (far left), named after Sir Henry, but originally part of the late 14th-century defences.*
BELOW *From the park the house looks even larger than it really is, since there is much space between the narrow wings. Penshurst has a collegiate layout, and the roof of the mediaeval hall dominates the whole complex of later buildings like the hall of many an Oxford or Cambridge college.*

Casa de Pilatos *Seville Spain c.1510*

This house lies in the centre of Seville. It is not, as one would expect of a ducal town-house elsewhere, squared off by streets and withdrawn behind railings and a formal forecourt, but fights for space in the tangle of little alleys which make Seville a stranger's nightmare. You can have visited the Casa de Pilatos three or four times, and still get lost trying to find it a fifth. Then suddenly the entrance appears in a slight swelling of a winding street – a classical archway with an inscription recording that the house was built at the beginning of the 16th century by Enriquez de Ribera, first Marquis of Tarifa.

The name 'Pilate's House' was given to it a little later because it was assumed that the Marquis, who had just returned from the Holy Land, was influenced by what he had seen of the Procurator of Judaea's house in Jerusalem, and based his own upon it. This theory was never endorsed by the Marquis himself, but the legend stuck, and the house became the start of a simulated Via Dolorosa, or Way of the Cross, which wound through Seville. What more appropriate beginning could it have than 'Pilate's House'? In fact, all mediaeval Seville recalls Jerusalem. The heat in midsummer is so intense that the houses are built close together for mutual shade, and the gardens and courts are kept small and hidden. Every house of any size has its *patio,* and the Casa de Pilatos is simply a magnification and duplication of the arrangements of smaller houses throughout the city. Instead of coming up for air, you went down for it. The winter quarters were on the first floor, the summer quarters at ground level, for only there could running water, the shade of trees and the cool of secluded rooms be found and enjoyed.

The house is apparently Moorish, yet it was built 250 years after St Ferdinand recaptured Seville from the Moors in 1248. This is one of the strangest aspects of Renaissance Spain. Most people, on first seeing the Alcazar or the great private houses of Seville, would assume that they had been built, like the Alhambra at Granada, for Arab grandees. But the style persisted long after the Arabs had been expelled or Christianised. It was found convenient and decorative. There are Gothic features in the Casa de

ABOVE *The house is entered through this classical archway, bearing the heads of two Roman emperors carved in Genoa, with Gothic openwork roundels above, and an inscription recording the building of the house.* OPPOSITE *A superb ironwork gate separates the outer court from the central patio.*

OPPOSITE *From an archway at the level of the roof-terraces one looks across Seville towards the Giralda, the graceful campanile beside the cathedral which was by origin a Moorish minaret.*

'The galleries are on two storeys, serving either as connecting arcades or as places in which to sit; and you can look, or talk, from one to another over the tops of palm-trees.'

OVERLEAF, LEFT *A corner of the central patio. A two-headed Janus watches over the fountain, and in the angle of the unequal arches is a statue of Pallas armed. The main rooms lie behind the arcades on each storey, the winter suite above, the summer suite below. 'Instead of coming up for air, you went down for it.'*
OVERLEAF, RIGHT *'So faithful is the imitation, that it requires a close look to discover that an apparent inscription in Arabic is in fact a simple patterning with no meaning.'*

Pilatos, like the vaulting of the chapel ceiling, and classical features, like the entrance gateway and the statuary. But it is still 'Arab' enough to strike one as oriental, not southern Mediterranean, and to have made a suitable setting for many scenes in the film of 'Lawrence of Arabia'.

This 'Moorishness' consists most obviously in the layout and the ornamentation. Large rooms, almost windowless, almost doorless, open on to galleries running round three or four sides of a court, and between them are gardens bursting with short-lived flowers of alarming exuberance and colour. Water plays on tile, and is fed along rivulets to different parts of the open courts. The galleries are on two storeys, serving either as connecting arcades or as places in which to sit, and you can look, or talk, from one to another over the tops of palm-trees. The house faces inwards. It has no façades except on to the inner courts, and its architectural features are not symmetrical. The arches of the main patio, for instance, are all of different sizes, when it would have been scarcely more difficult to make them identical. The plan, drawn out on paper, looks illogical, like that of some early Mycenaean or Cretan palace, and one expects part of it to be reserved for women, part for eunuchs. But this illogicality is unnoticed in fact. It is a house for slow movement from one part to another, seeking always refuge from the sun, a change of shadow, a change of breeze, or a change of one cool surface for another. It has something of the Roman *atrium*. Pilate's house may not have been so very different after all.

The decoration is very obviously modelled on Arab prototypes. So faithful is the imitation, that it requires a close look to discover that an apparent inscription in Arabic is in fact a simple patterning with no meaning. The archways are fretted into rows of jagged teeth against the sky, and the ceilings are coffered and honeycombed so that they become at the same time heavy and porous. The walls are covered to half or all their height by Azulejo tiles, painted in bright colours with floral and other patterns. There is almost no furniture, but seats are contrived in the window-embrasures and a single table is often enough to make a room habitable.

None of this, let it be repeated, was built by or for Arabs. The Ribera family, later Dukes of Medinaceli, who still own it, were Spaniards. They adopted the Islamic style, but they also adapted it. The whole house is a modification of the Mudéjar manner. There is not an arch of horseshoe shape; all are either semicircular or pointed. The window and door openings are fitted with excellent iron-work in Renaissance patterns. The chapel is Christian in spirit as well as in purpose. In the main court, a two-sided Janus head occupies the central position, and four classical statues, larger than life, stand in the angles. In circular niches round the walls sit busts of Roman Emperors. All of this occidentalises the house. It is not a Renaissance house in fancy dress. It is a fusion between two worlds, which having fought each other, learnt from each other. It is a way of living, partly traditional, partly experimental, governed by climate and the compression of space. Room has to be found for the garden within the house, and

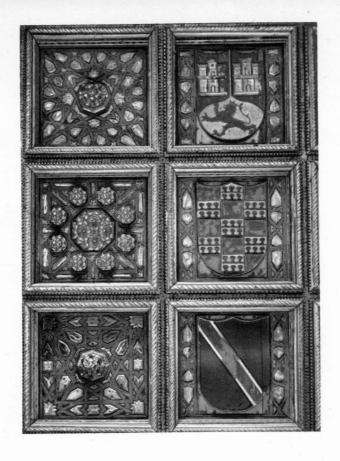

ABOVE *The brilliant coffering of the ceilings includes the often repeated arms of Castille (top right).*

OPPOSITE *The great staircase, like much else in the house, is a Renaissance adaptation of the Moorish style, and climbs in broad flights between walls of coloured tiles.*

the winter quarters on the first floor were duplicated by the summer quarters below.

The Casa de Pilatos is usually praised for its decoration. The expanse of tiling is indeed almost unequalled in Spain, but there is too much of it. The repetition of the effect, whatever the variations of detail, creates tedium, as if every room in a house were papered in the same pattern, or worse still, the pattern changed for another several times in a single stretch of wall. The staircase, for instance, is less beautiful than interesting, although it is often quoted as one of the wonders of southern Spain, since the tiles climb in big squares up its large and rather gloomy well to a high semi-domed ceiling which is in half-darkness. Nor is the stucco excellent of its kind. It lacks crispness ; it lacks translucency ; and where it has become shabby, it is tawdry and dull. Nowhere in the Casa de Pilatos is there detail as magical as in the Alhambra, perhaps because the style was at last dying out, and because the palace of Granada stood on a hill-top exposed to the light instead of in a low-lying city where every effort was made to exclude it.

The pleasure of the house is in its planning. It is a beautiful place for its compactness, its privacy, its internal courts, its gardens. Still, today, it is a wonderful house for a large party in summer, when the main patio is converted into a ballroom and the rooms around it into drawing-rooms and buffets. From the galleries overhead the less self-confident can look down without being seen themselves. It must always have been so. It is a house for escape – escape from the torturing sun, escape from noise, escape from other human beings. At the same time it is a house for congregation, for in what more pleasant way can a large number of guests be dispersed than through a chain of courtyards and gardens, where vine-leaves lick the curves of an Islamic arch?

Azay-le-Rideau *Indre-et-Loire France 1518-27*

The staircase is not immediately recognisable as such. It looks more like superimposed pairs of windows, and when they were glassed in (see the early 19th-century print above), it seemed even more so. But the glass has now rightly been removed to restore the original appearance of this frontage as finished in about 1527. The staircase extends the whole depth of the wing. It was the first in France to be incorporated in the building, instead of contained spirally in an attached tower.

The *rideau* of the château's name has nothing to do with 'curtain', but is derived from a certain Ridel d'Azay who built a fortress here on the River Indre, halfway between Tours and Chinon, in the 12th century. In 1418 it was burnt to the ground by order of the Dauphin, the future Charles VII, who considered that his troops had been insulted by the village-people. A few years later Joan of Arc rode this way, and it seems that she persuaded Charles to permit the rebuilding of the little fortress. Only a stone or two of it is still visible.

This mediaeval introduction would be quite irrelevant to an account of Azay-le-Rideau were it not that the Middle Ages still seem very close to the place. The defensive water-works, the romantic skyline of the château, its name, the surrounding countryside littered with ruined keeps and noble abbeys – all form a bridge between our own day and that. The Azay which we know was built between 1518 and 1527. It could scarcely occupy a more central and important position in French history and French architecture.

A short avenue of chestnuts leads off the village street to the entrance of the house. The avenue is tall and finely shaped like a nave, and at the far end of it you see part of the façade – but a carefully selected part, for everything is excluded from this view but the entrance staircase, as if it had been the builder's object to focus attention first and last upon this feature. If so, it was a legitimate boast, since the staircase at Azay-le-Rideau is indeed a wonderful conception beautifully executed, and it can stand for much else in Touraine dating from the beginning of the French Renaissance. It is, in the first place, most original. Until then, main staircases had been spiral and enclosed in towers separate from the house. At Azay the flights are straight, not winding, and the whole staircase is incorporated in the house, its face flush with the main walls. It is built four storeys high, in pairs of open arches

The exterior detail of the staircase is a lovely mixture of Gothic with Renaissance motifs, and the close-up of one of the bays OPPOSITE *gives an idea of the richness of the sculptor's invention directed by a woman of taste, Philippe Lesbahy, wife of Gilles Berthelot, the builder of Azay. Below is the salamander, crest of François I, who later appropriated the château.*

with a very elaborate pediment surmounting the uppermost pair. From outside it acts as an elegant frontispiece; from inside as a series of open arcades on the different floors. As you mount it, you are half-enclosed, as if in a porch, and the rain and wind can blow through the arches into the lobbies to freshen them, for everything within is of stone and there is nothing to spoil. On sunny days, the separate floors become loggias, and tempt the visitor to halt at each as he ascends and look back across the bridges and the water below. The idea is very simple, but has seldom been imitated. Why not? Why not make a staircase an internal and external feature, like a window, and while affording immediate shelter, delay by this enticing method the moment of entry into the body of the house itself?

Decoratively, too, the staircase is exceedingly charming, because the proportions are good and the stone-carving is as suggestive from a distance as it is pleasing from close-up. The monumental gable at the stairhead stands away from the roof like a tiara, and framing the open arches up the full height of the wall are columns in the Italian manner, sometimes broken by Gothic sculptured niches. What a lovely marriage between two styles!

The house was dedicated to François I and his queen, Claude de France, by inserting at the level of the first and third floors on the outside of the staircase a salamander and an ermine, their respective badges. The King's motto was also inscribed: *Nutrisco et Extinguo*, 'I nurture and I abolish'. This was a terrible prediction to fasten on the face of the house while it was building. No sooner was it finished in 1527 than its builder, Gilles Berthelot, Treasurer-General of France, was implicated in the Semblançay financial scandals and obliged to flee the country. His new house, which he had scarcely seen, was confiscated by François I and

The south wing, which drops straight into the water of the Indre. 'Azay is not a castle surrounded by a moat, but a galleon moored in a river's centre . . . The mediaeval elements of castles are traceable but immensely refined . . . It is Renaissance, but not classical. It is original, but incorporates the French tradition. It is a wonderful house.'

given to a new favourite. No place recalls more vividly than Azay-le-Rideau the dreadful reversals of human fortunes. It changed hands many times before becoming the property of the State in 1905. But life was never more uncertain than at the period when it was built, and it is remarkable that a house of such serenity should be the creation of a man whose ambition exposed him to constant risks.

Some have explained the 'femininity' of Azay by attributing much of its design to Berthelot's wife, Philippe Lesbahy. This is flattering to her, but unlikely. The main lines would have been laid out, like Chenonceaux, its neighbour and contemporary, in the style which the King himself had made fashionable by his additions to Blois. The water of the Indre was a natural asset, both defensively and scenically, for the château is surrounded by it, half-moat, half water-garden, and on all but the entrance side, where a bridge leads to a forecourt, the walls drop sheer into the water. It is, in fact, an island, and the constant flowing of the river past it and around it gives it a romantic quality which is further enhanced by the amazing silhouette of the roof-line. Azay is not a castle surrounded by a moat, but a galleon moored in a river's centre. It has been said that it was never finished, and that Berthelot, had it not been for his disgrace, would have added two more wings to the forecourt, thus completely enclosing it. This theory is questionable, because two of the turrets, at the extremities of the present L, would have prevented the squaring-off of the courtyard by extra wings. In any case, it would have darkened the place and given it too formidable an aspect and too great a size. The fact that it is open to view on all sides, whether accidental or deliberate, greatly increases its charm.

As you move around the garden, crossing various bridges over running streams so divided that you are never quite certain which is the main channel and which are artificial cuts, you see the mass of the house lying low on the water and sheltered from the town of Azay by a thick growth of trees. As far as the roof-line it is fairly plain – the walls divided into rectangular panels by vertical and horizontal bands and the windows neatly transomed into crosses. At the corners are mediaeval towers transformed into Renaissance turrets, corbelled out from the wall just above the water surface. The flourish is reserved for the roof-level. Here all the features, including the roof itself, break into spikes and finials. The turrets have caps as slim and tapering as those of pagodas; the dormers are lovely little set-pieces of decorative masonry; the false machicolations provide an embroidered hem below them; and from each end of the roof-ridge rise tall finials topped by stately figures in lead. In all this the mediaeval elements of castles are traceable but immensely refined. Some, like the machicolations, were quite useless, since any molten liquids poured through them would only fall on the protruding string-courses below. The parapet walk has become a decorative balustrade. Slit windows have been enlarged and spaced symmetrically. A revolution in design has taken place. It owes little except superficial ornament to the Italians. It is Renaissance, but not classical. It is original, but incorporates the French tradition. It is a wonderful house.

ABOVE *One of the main reception rooms on the ground floor. Great emphasis was given to the fireplaces throughout the house, to compensate for the sparseness of furniture and the bare stone walls. The furniture is not original to the house, which passed through many hands during its long history, but has been brought here from other French national collections.* TOP *The Salle des Fêtes, the largest room in the house, is hung with 17th-century tapestries, representing scenes from the life of Constantine.* OPPOSITE *The overmantel in the Grand Salon is a magnificent Renaissance manifestation of the salamander of François I, the king who rewarded the loyalty of his subject, Gilles Berthelot, by confiscating Azay almost as soon as it was built.*

Inside, the visitor must not expect too much. The hand of the Renaissance touched the exteriors of houses before the interiors, and none of the elaborate stone-carving on the face of the staircase, for instance, is reproduced within the rooms. There is barely a moulded cornice in the whole place. We are given some stupendous fireplaces, complete with salamander and ermine (hideous animals with which to cohabit), and the rooms are of good proportion, if rather too big: even a four-poster looks lost in the corner of a bedroom large enough for a banquet. A further disadvantage is that Azay is not inhabited. A platoon of guides and guardians, however well-meaning, is no substitute for hosts, nor tourists for guests; while the furniture, loaned from the reserve collections of Paris museums, though correct in date and in style, seems not to belong to the house because it is never used. This is a familiar dilemma. Rob a house of indigenous life, and you rob it of affection.

However, Azay-le-Rideau is without question one of the most beautiful houses in the world. It had, as we now understand the term, no architect. It was experimental. It was fumbling for something entirely new, for a refinement of which no model existed, except in other houses like Chenonceaux which were being built simultaneously nearby. Yet Azay is greater than Chenonceaux, with which it is often compared, since it is more compact, being built all at one time and all of a piece, while the famous arched wing of Chenonceaux was added over the Cher half a century later. And though fumbling, Azay succeeds in expressing the mood which only exists during rare periods of cultural rebirth – a mood of wide-eyed wonder, almost of innocence, of hesitation and yet of daring too. To suppose that such evanescent human qualities can be expressed in stone and lead and reflected in water may be thought exaggerated, and perhaps we read into Azay-le-Rideau ideas of gentility which never occurred to its tough, unscrupulous builders. If so, it is a legitimate error, for one of the pleasures given by so beautiful a building is the pleasure of attributing to its builders the very impressions which we derive from it after the passage of four hundred and fifty years.

Sarospatak *near Miskolc Hungary c.1540-1610*

TOP *A sketch of the fortified town of Sarospatak in about 1650. The River Bodrog is in the foreground, the castle on the left (with a steep roof, now disappeared, capping its central tower), and the parish church on the right.* ABOVE *It is already obvious from across the River Bodrog that two later wings have been added to a mediaeval keep. The stone fort in the centre was built in about 1260 by the kings of Hungary. The wing on the right was added by Peter Perényi in 1526, and the wing on the left by the Rakoczis in the 17th century.* OPPOSITE *Fortifications which have clearly stood up to much alteration. The original 'fighting floor' is marked by the row of gun-ports. Above it is a Renaissance window inserted later; and below, part of the early 16th-century bastion built by the Italian Alessandro da Vedano for the Perényis.*

The great plain of Hungary makes little appeal to the westerner brought up to regard green valleys, meadows and forests as the only true solace for harassed urban minds. It is very hot or very cold, and always very flat. But the Hungarians themselves love their plain with fierce patriotism, and the absence of the gentler courtesies of nature has given the people their courage and determination. Certainly their rough life and turbulent history have left a mark on their architecture, but Sarospatak, lying in the eastern part of the country, only a score of miles from its border with Russia, is an excellent example of a castle transformed by more peaceful conditions and the finger-tip influence of the Italian Renaissance into a pleasant house. In this book it stands as an outpost of the western world, as it did in history. It is fairly rugged architecture, even in its latest phase, but it is remarkable that it should have come to look like this at all.

From across the River Bodrog we see a 13th-century stone keep flanked by two white wings of an obviously later date. The whole group of buildings still wears the appearance of a castle, and it is not difficult to spot at this first glance that the keep was once the strong-point of a completely walled town. From its battlements you look eastwards to a low horizon brought nearer by haze. Below are the types of room which are common to mediaeval fortresses throughout Europe. The same dangers, the same needs, produced more or less the same buildings, until art began to interfere. This is not to say that the rooms are charmless. There is a cleanliness about hewn stone which is always attractive, and the keep of Sarospatak is particularly rich in small closets, window-seats and unexpected mediaeval comforts which show that the big rooms were reserved for the big occasions, and that the pleasure of privacy was well recognised. But it remains a fortress. Sandwiched between the upper and lower floors is a fighting-floor. It is Sarospatak's most startling feature. A low

44

gallery rings the keep internally, leaving frequent apertures for weapons through the 14-foot thick walls, so that every part of the approaches to the castle could be kept under observation and fire from this elevated dungeon. Crouching at one of the openings (it is much too low to stand), one can imagine the dust-clouds raised by hostile hooves approaching, and looking around, find some comfort in the immense walls built by the earliest Rakoczis, with whose family Sarospatak will always be associated.

In the early 16th century the softening process began. A wing was thrown out eastwards from the keep, and attached to it was an external staircase which climbs in the arched Renaissance manner to the first floor, forming what is perhaps the prettiest feature of the whole house, for the arches are continued as a gallery, dated 1542, linking the wing to the keep. Three equal windows, side by side, admit light to the ground-floor of this wing. They are decorated with stunted capitals, medallions and architraves which illustrate in a fascinating way the first impact of Italian motifs on distant Hungary, no more crude and no less vigorous than the same motifs adapted and equally misunderstood by contemporary craftsmen in Britain.

The two other wings date from the early 17th century, forming a courtyard of roughly diamond shape onto which the old tower looks down. The walls are faced with clean yellow stucco and have a pleasant, if rather too conventional, appearance when

BELOW *A Renaissance gallery and staircase link the mediaeval keep of Sarospatak to the wing built by the Perényis in the early 16th century.* BOTTOM *A triple-window in the Perényi wing is convincing proof of the endeavours of Hungarian artists to follow European trends in decoration.* OPPOSITE *In the 17th century, eastern Hungary lost touch with artistic developments in the rest of Europe, and it is clear from this window, dated 1643, that the local style has grown rigid.*

seen alongside the sturdy functionalism of the keep. Inside there is much to admire. The working room of the Rakoczis was formed out of an angle-turret, with windows on four sides of the octagon and a dome which sends down ribs between the windows forming panels which are spangled with painted flowers. In the centre of the dome is a rose, so that the lord could work peacefully *sub rosa*. This little room is one indication of the family's sense of domestic comfort; but another is the lord's bed, also preserved in the house, a thick baulk of timber worn clean through at one end by the scraping of the spurs which he was too tired or too vigilant to remove when he went to rest.

Other Renaissance and 17th-century rooms exist, but almost all of them were changed when the 18th-century owners introduced their own conceptions of refinement. Today the house is a museum. It contains some excellent historical maps and exhibits, and some rooms are furnished in the style of the different periods through which the house has passed. No number of tourists, no quantity of notice-boards or roped-off gangways, can obliterate the unity of Sarospatak. It is clearly a house which, like an oak, has stood firm and grown.

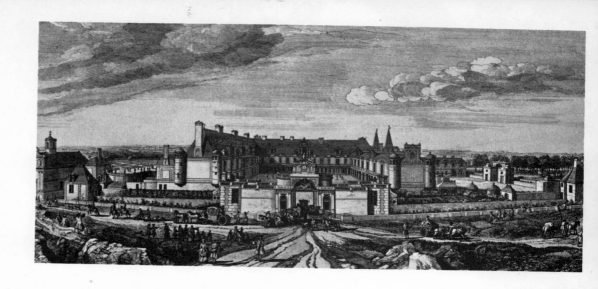

Château d'Anet *Eure-et-Loir France 1547-50*

Anyone who happened to be driving westward from Paris towards Normandy through the small town of Anet would stop the car with a squeal of brakes and pleasure at the first sight of the château's extraordinary appearance from the road. But few people come upon Anet by chance. It is worth not merely a detour, in *Michelin* language, but a day's expedition. Yet when you get there, there is not all that much to see. An entrance gateway, the wing of a once-larger château, two chapels and a view of trees and water – that is almost all. Why then does it enjoy such fame, and make so lasting an impression ? There are two answers : its associations and its architectural distinction. Anet was built by the greatest architect of the French Renaissance, Philibert de l'Orme, for its most famous woman, Diane de Poitiers. In later generations it suffered abominably from neglect and destruction. but these disasters were always followed by periods of rescue and renewed brilliance as it passed from a poorer hand to a richer. Everybody wanted to visit Anet because Anet had been visited by everybody before. Its fame grew by accretion, and its disasters are today almost as great an attraction as its triumphs. The mutilation of the house is not a deformity dating from birth, but a limb lost in battle. Its nobility is still very obvious, and enough remains of the original for one to be able to imagine the whole.

The story of Henri II's passion for Diane de Poitiers, which was the origin of the Château d'Anet, is so extraordinary that it must briefly be retold. Born on the very last day of the 15th century, she was married at the age of fifteen to a man forty years older than herself, Louis de Brézé, Sénéchal of Normandy, among whose possessions was a sad but sturdy castle at Anet. He died there in 1531. His widow was much admired at the Court of François I, and her greatest admirer was the Dauphin, Henri, aged 15 when Diane was 33. Henri married Catherine de Medici in 1533, but his love for Diane was unabated and openly acknowledged. The three of

ABOVE *The château in the 17th century, when it stood complete. The chapel stood behind the right-hand wing, to which it was connected, and only the two pyramids of its façade are here visible.* OPPOSITE *The château was built between 1547 and 1552 by Philibert de l'Orme for Diane de Poitiers. The entrance gate alone is an astonishing architectural novelty for that date, but it also served a purpose : it provided lodgings for the porter, and balconies from which the ladies could watch the departure of the hunt and its return.*

them – widow-mistress, husband-lover, child-bride – shared each others' lives and castles, not without a certain jealousy on Catherine's part, but a jealousy tempered by Diane's discretion. She encouraged Henri to be a dutiful husband, calculating, perhaps, that if there were no children of the marriage, her own position at court could paradoxically be weakened, for he might be tempted to seek another wife, who might be less complaisant.

Diane was a remarkable woman. Contemporaries spoke of her beauty as something never seen on earth before, and their tributes are more convincing than the surviving portraits, which show us a woman plump of cheek and body, whose preference for being painted half-naked was, to our eyes, an error both of taste and judgement. She had a dominating, but not charmless, manner. She was an excellent manager, fond of the arts (especially of music), with a strong will and a mind and physical energy which were a match for men's. She was ambitious, calculating and formidable. When to these qualities you add the capacity to enslave a king nearly twenty years younger than herself, it is not surprising that Diane de Poitiers was a person whom history remembers with awe, and that when in 1547 she came to rebuild her house, it was a house such as men had never previously imagined.

Philibert de l'Orme, her architect, was the son of a master mason of Lyons and one of the few Frenchmen of the day to have studied on the spot the ancient and new buildings of Rome. He brought to Anet a technician's grasp of what could be done by the cutting and suspension of stone, and an artist's understanding that the new architecture of Italy was more than a matter of surface decoration, but involved a reinterpretation of the principles that had produced buildings like the Pantheon and the aqueducts. Given the chance to rebuild Anet for the challenging woman who was in all but name Queen of France, he was not content merely to reshuffle the traditional elements of tower, turret and dormer, but began to play with new arrangements of new shapes, without slavishly imitating what he had seen in Rome. He was not contemptuous of the French tradition. He wanted to refashion it, using fresh ideas to create fresh patterns.

The result can be seen from the road outside. The entrance

TOP *One of the innumerable panels which survive to testify to the love between Diane de Poitiers and Henri II – bows and moons and Hs and Ds – all this in a house where the King was a frequent visitor with his wife Catherine de Medici.* ABOVE *Diane de Poitiers (1499-1566). A portrait in the house surrounded by the emblems of her name, a bow and the crescent moon, and the triumphant assertion of Henri II's love for her, 'I have conquered the conqueror of all'.* OPPOSITE *The surviving wing seen from across the water on the far side of the house.*

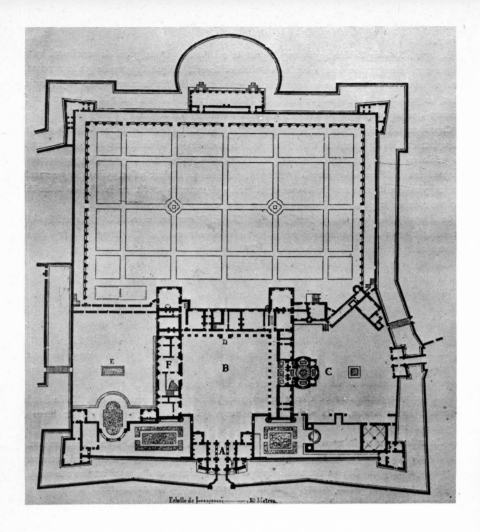

buildings of the château incorporate an astonishing range of cubes and curves, not one of which, except the moat which is lost below, was traditional. The combination of brick with stone and black marble introduced the idea that colour and texture can be important attributes of buildings ; the central archway with two smaller arches and Doric columns on each side was the Roman triumphal arch transformed ; the pierced balustrades, arranged in straight lengths alternating with hoops, were boldly experimental ; the bronze group of hounds and stag on the summit of the pyramid, together with Cellini's Nymph in the pediment below (the original is in the Louvre), was for France a wholly new method of employing sculpture on buildings. But this is not all. The front of Anet is as diversified and challenging as an exhibition. There are two terminal pavilions, and between them and the gateway, terraces on different levels, incorporating gardens, rounded steps and inexplicable humps and elaborate sarcophagi which turn out to be chimneys. The arrangement is both playful and monumental. It cannot be called wholly successful as a work of architecture, since it lacks cohesion ; it is not immediately plain whether its purpose is to impress or to amuse ; there is something bizarre, almost oriental, in the profusion of these different shapes. 'This astonishing structure,' wrote Anthony Blunt, de l'Orme's biographer, 'has, as far as I know, neither predecessor nor successor . . . It is thought of as a series of blocks of masonry, playing against each other almost in the manner of functionalist architecture.' It puzzles the visitor ; it makes him eager to know what can lie behind.

The plan makes clear the relationship between the original house and the present house. The latter is shown in heavy blocking. A. The entrance. B. The cour d'honneur (originally enclosed on all four sides). C. The chapel. F. The surviving wing of the château. Behind the buildings is the vast parterre of which there is now hardly any relic. BELOW Almost all the surviving parts of the château are in this photograph: the entrance archway (left foreground), the one remaining wing of the house (left background), the chapel (right).

What lies behind is only a relic of what there was originally, but from illustrations made before the greater part was destroyed in the Revolution and from pieces surviving at Anet and elsewhere, one can reconstruct exactly the appearance of the château at its prime. It formed a courtyard with a central building facing the entrance archway, and a wing on either side. Beyond were courts, and a large enclosed garden behind the central building. For a semi-royal palace, it was not particularly large. Much space was used in forming open colonnades along the ground floor of two of the three wings, and a single room, Diane's long gallery, on the first floor of the right-hand wing. When the King stayed there with his mistress, he was accompanied by a large entourage and often by his Queen. They must have been inconveniently cramped. But surviving accounts of Anet, both in this and succeeding centuries, suggest that it was a place where much pleasure was extracted and given. The entertainments were on a princely scale. The hunting forest of Dreux lay close by ; nearer at hand there were water-gardens and tennis-pavilions which could absorb an entire court. One should imagine the courtiers dispersed for the night in the surrounding villages and châteaux, while Anet itself was reserved for the curious *ménage à trois* which gave the place its spirit and its fame.

There was no playing-down of Diane's role in this frolic. Anet was raised as a temple to the King's love for her. His initial is found entwined with hers on every part of the building, H with D. More often it is D alone, or symbols of the goddess Diana. For was not her status both excused and enhanced by identifying her, half playfully, half mystically, with the Roman goddess of the moon and the chase ? Hence we find the crescent moon, or bow, arrows and a quiver, or triangles (the Greek delta) singly or doubled to form stars, applied in paint or wood or metal or plaster to any surface or projection which would take them – on ceilings, on floors, on furniture, on exterior walls, on the very cross above the chapel and on the tomb in which Diane was laid (where the arrows are shown with heads snapped and the bow unstrung), until one begins to see a crescent in every archway and a delta in every pediment, and the vigour and enchantment of this woman, carried across the centuries, transforms an outrage into a glorious fantasy.

She built two chapels, one attached to the eastern wing of the château, and one, finished after her death, in which her tomb should lie. The former was a more wonderful invention by de l'Orme even than his entrance-building, for it was the first chapel in France to be domed, and as if this were not innovation enough, it was coffered internally as no other dome has ever been, sculpted in ever-diminishing diamonds arranged on inclined planes of fantastic geometrical subtlety, but with an effect of whipped clouds, greatly increasing the lightness and apparent height of this little building from within. Outside its fantasy is less successful, for the two stone pyramids topped by gilded armillary spheres do not sit happily alongside the dome and the cupola, and the latter is too heavy for the former, as the cross is for both. The laws of proportion which de l'Orme so greatly emphasised in his architectural writings seem strangely neglected here. Once again, one appreciates the ebullience of his experiment without quite understanding its purpose.

The dome of the chapel remains as Philibert de l'Orme built it, 'sculpted in ever-diminishing diamonds arranged on inclined planes of fantastic geometrical subtlety, but with an effect of whipped clouds, greatly increasing the lightness and apparent height of this little building from within.'

The same cannot be said of the main buildings. They were strong, substantial and well-balanced. Only one wing survives *in situ*, but the frontispiece of the main block was re-erected in Paris as part of the Ecole des Beaux-Arts, where it can still be seen. The surviving wing was considerably altered externally and internally in the late 17th century, when Anet belonged to Louis-Joseph, Duc de Vendôme, and it is as a 17th-century building that it should now be considered rather than as Philibert de l'Orme's. It is with something like guilt that the visitor stands amazed at the beauty of the Duke's hall and stairway, completed in the 1680s, for the transformation of this interior was vandalism of an historic work of art. Nevertheless, Anet has always been a place where innovation was honoured and convention ridiculed, and this great stairway, spilling like a duchess's train across the black and white marble floor, is breathtakingly beautiful in its arrogance. The walls rise to the height of the roof, with Corinthian pilasters and busts of Roman emperors standing high up on brackets, while above and below are doors decorated in butter-gold on ivory panels, the lower pair flanked by two superb *torchères* of Roman soldiers, helmeted, but wigged below their gleaming helmets.

Anet experienced one of its brilliant revivals during the period of Vendôme's ownership. It became the equivalent of England's Blenheim. Le Nôtre transformed the garden as the Duke did the house, and both left relics – the great canal, the great staircase – which are in a sense out of scale and character with Diane's impertinent little château, even more so now that half the château has vanished. But it is the fate of Anet to be a *grand mutilé*. The present owners, Monsieur and Madame de Yturbe, occupy the surviving wing, surrendering half their house to a staircase and a vast Salle des Gardes, and half their park and garden to water-works which rival Versailles', yet the life which they live there is comfortable and secluded. Even though you can scarcely put your hand on a door-knob without finding it to be shaped like the crescent moon, or twitch a curtain straight without revealing some episode in the life of Diana, human or mythological, that incomparable Diane is still a tolerable woman to live with, as Henri II and Catherine de Medici found four hundred years ago.

The hall and stairway with its magnificent wrought-iron balustrade, constructed by the Duc de Vendôme in the 1680s. 'This great stairway, spilling like a duchess's train across the black and white marble floor, is breathtakingly beautiful in its arrogance.' In this same hall stand the two torchères *of Roman soldiers (*RIGHT*) wearing wigs beneath their helmets.*

58

Villa Foscari *Malcontenta Italy c.1558*

OPPOSITE *The garden-front of the villa (of which a detail is shown* ABOVE*) is a very subtle composition, but is less familiar than the entrance-front illustrated overleaf. It reveals by its fenestration something of the interior design. The six-light central window is that of the main room, the upper three lights following the curve of the vaulted ceiling to break the pediment externally. Only one of the original chimneys, typically Venetian, survived when A.C. Landsberg acquired the property in 1925.* TOP *The front façade, illustrated by Palladio in his Four Books of Architecture, 1570.*

The house was built in the late 1550s by Andrea Palladio. This bald statement immediately suggests a whole range of associations. The decade marked the height of Palladio's achievement as a designer of country houses. The Villa Foscari is contemporary with his Villa Barbaro at Maser and the Villa Emo at Fanzolo; it followed within a few years his Villa Capra (the 'Rotonda') and the Palazzo Chiericati at Vicenza. All of them, lying in a semicircle of 25 miles' radius from Padua, survive. No group of buildings by a single architect has so strongly attracted later generations, particularly in the north. You can see Palladio's ideas reproduced in England, Ireland, Scotland, the United States and even Russia, and not only in grand country seats, for until the last twenty or thirty years the Palladian style was an almost instinctive choice for institutional buildings where an impression of aristocratic stability was required. So familiar has Palladianism become to our eyes that we take it for granted, but to contemporaries houses like that at Malcontenta must have represented an extraordinary break with tradition, especially for great Venetian families like the Foscari, for whom it was built.

Palladio built as he imagined the Romans might have built had their civilization persisted until the 16th century. He guessed (for excavation of Roman villa-sites was then rudimentary) that they made great use of columns in their façades, reproducing on a more domestic scale the dignified approaches to their temples. We now know that he guessed correctly, for although it is often stated that the Romans did not adopt the temple motif for

private houses, wall-paintings at Pompeii and elsewhere have made it clear that they did. A fresco in the House of Lucretius Fronto at Pompeii, for example, illustrates a raised portico at a villa's centre which might have been taken as the model for the entrance to the Villa Foscari, while others show arcades curving away from the main block, sometimes in two galleried storeys, just as Palladio designed for his villas at Meledo and Fratta Polesine. But he was not a sleek imitator of the antique. He had strong original views on what made a house decorative, habitable and imposing, and he drew from the Romans only such ideas as suited his villas, and the principles of mathematical harmony which he considered 'the true ornament of all who possess noble and virtuous spirits'. Of these principles he believed the Romans to have been the discoverers and grandest exponents. The Villa Foscari is a superb example of his adaptation and transformation of their style.

It lies on the Brenta canal, some eight miles by road from Venice, set back only thirty yards from the water's edge, but aslant to it, like a chair slightly turned away, so that if you approach it by the canal, or by the road which runs along the opposite bank, you first see its side elevation. The house seems shy, withdrawn. Its mysteriousness is now enhanced by the trees which shield it from the public road opposite. Willows dangle their tresses to the surface of the water and suspend a leafy screen through which the house is glimpsed like a stage-setting before the last gauze curtain is drawn aside and the lights turned up. How different from the unmasked brilliance of Venetian palaces!

Without its portico the house would be but a plain cube with excrescences on the roof. The overwhelming impression of this solemn portico draws every eye away from every other part. It is raised on a lofty podium, following the Roman tradition, but the steps are not wide and frontal like those of the Maison Carrée at Nîmes and other Roman temples, which Palladio adapted for the four entrances to the Rotonda, but are set with comparative modesty on either side of the portico and rise two flights in the form of an L, leaving the face of the podium free for a lower entrance-door and flanking windows. Even in its present roughened condition, lacking the balusters (which may only have been added in the 17th century) and with the stucco flaked from the underlying brick of the lower walls and columns, the approach still creates the sense of wonder and anticipation which Palladio intended. 'In all my villas,' he wrote, 'I have put a frontispiece on the forward façade where the principal doors are, because such frontispieces show the entrance to the house, and add very much to the grandeur and magnificence of the work, the front being thus made more eminent than the other parts.' Require your visitors on landing from their gondolas or barges to mount an elevated platform, gradually enfold them with great pillars, give them a sense of privilege by leaving the lesser entrance below, and you will have prepared them for the dignified welcome that awaits them and the patrician serenity of the interior. Such was the idea. But as they waited for admission within the portico, visitors must instinctively have turned round to look back on the

The entrance-front, with (OPPOSITE) the Brenta canal at its foot. Willows have been planted to screen the house from the public road, which runs along the near bank of the canal, but the restoration of this front has been confined to the minimum repairs.

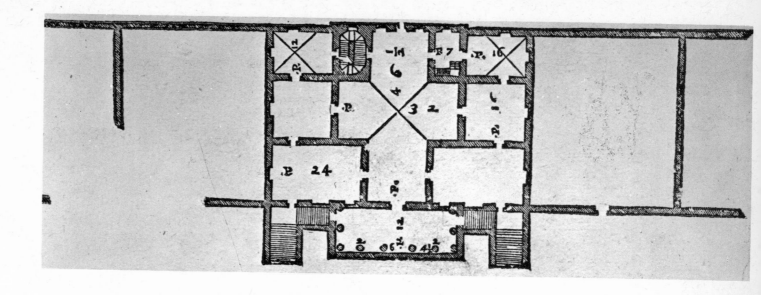

canal. There below them was a simple forecourt, and the water-way busy with propelled or horse-towed traffic. The columns half-screened the world outside. Even before entering the house new arrivals found themselves within a faintly numinous en-closure. Perhaps, too, as today, they dined there on warm even-ings, partly outside, partly inside, while the stars and lights of little boats moved slowly across the intercolumniations.

The great double doors are of wood, almost barn-like. A single row of bricks forms the simplest possible threshold, dividing the floor of the porch from the floor of the *sala* just inside. This com-bination of homeliness with soaring architecture would never have been acceptable in Venice, but it is repeated throughout the villa and was clearly deliberate. Brick is faced with stucco on the outside, floors are of the original tile, or, in the *piano nobile*, of a marble composition known as *pavimento Veneziano*. There is almost no moulded decoration in the entire house. Its architec-ture still gives it an air of cultivated grandeur, but as the villa is not only in the country, but of the country, it is not surprising that once its days of glory were over, the Villa Foscari slipped back without loss of dignity to become a farmhouse, a corn-store and, in 1848, a billet for invading Austrian soldiery, before its perfections were rediscovered and restored.

There is no vestibule inside the outer door. You step straight into the central room which acted both as a reception room and as a corridor for access to the smaller rooms on either side. From outside you might have expected a large rectangular room with a flat beamed ceiling, running from front to back. Instead you find a cruciform, vaulted hall (the word *aula*, in Italian as in Latin, best expresses its nature), rising high into the centre of the house like a Roman bath-house and closed at the end opposite the en-trance by a great battery of windows, of which the upper three follow the curve of the vault. It is impossible to capture the ideal

65

proportions of this room by photography. You must be within it, able to move and turn around, running the eye up the knife-edged groins of the converging arches where 'nave' meets 'transept' (the form is basilican, and ecclesiastical terms fuse naturally with secular) to a ceiling that always seems to be in slight motion, even at the central point where an iron ring suggests that a chandelier may once have swung. It is very simply furnished. Low sofas cushioned in soft colours occupy the angles, window-seats are arranged behind unobtrusive balustrades, and two golden globes and an octagonal table stand in the centre. That is almost all. The variety of this perfectly symmetrical room is created not by objects disposed about it, but by the shadows of its recesses, of which some are always half-hidden from whatever position you choose to look. The eye is drawn now to the pattern of the concave vaults, now across to one or other of the seven doors, and always to the frescoes.

The Villa Foscari was decorated in fresco by Zellotti and Battista Franco as soon as the walls were ready to receive it. The attribution of some of the paintings to Veronese is less sure, though his influence is obvious. In the 19th century they were covered in whitewash, and when Bertie Landsberg bought the house in 1925, he began with infinite patience to remove it. Piece by piece the old frescoes were revealed, not in the pristine freshness of the wall-paintings by Veronese at Maser, for the whitewash had penetrated deeply, but as ghosts of their former richness, much as rose-petals are faded by conversion into pot-pourri. The walls have the appearance of tapestry softened by exposure. There are heroic, mythological and allegorical figures, each painted boldly before the plaster dried, and they are perhaps easier to live with in their present mottled state than when richly glowing. In addition, and even more effective, are the painted architectural features, possibly suggested and designed by Palladio himself. Painted Ionic columns, and in other rooms Corinthian, stand sentinel around the walls, and elaborate architraves and pediments crown the doors and windows, painted rather disturbingly in perspective, but so muted by their subsequent treatment that they merge perfectly with the un-ornamented architecture, and it is often difficult to be certain without close inspection whether a cornice or a beading is real or painted. The *trompe l'œil* continues to the ceilings. The frescoes are rightly considered, after the portico, to be the villa's second glory. They occur in every room on the main floor, consistent in their colouring and effect, but greatly varied in detail, scale and subject, even to little Venetian landscapes sketched with all the charm of hurried improvisation in two of the smaller rooms.

The family life of the house revolved around the *sala*. Below, at ground level, were the kitchens and store-rooms with their beautiful and varied vaulting; above, spare bedrooms and a central room as large as a normal hall. They are connected by tiny spiral staircases. But large as the *sala* is, there is still space on the *piano nobile* for six other rooms and small anterooms around it, all opening from it and into each other. With great ingenuity Palladio controlled the height of each of these *stanze* to suit its

The central part of the ceiling of the 'sala'. The frescoes, which Palladio attributed to Battista Franco, are allegories of Peace, Prosperity, Hospitality and similar themes. OPPOSITE *One of the two 'groteschi' cabinets on the main floor, probably painted by Zellotti or Franco. Ornaments of this kind became fashionable centuries before the discovery of the wall-paintings at Pompeii, to which they bear an obvious resemblance. In the lunette above the door is one of several idyllic Venetian landscapes.* BELOW *The Room of the Giants, one of the rooms opening off the 'sala', and so-called from the frescoes of Titans struck by Jupiter's thunderbolts among the ruins of Corinthian architecture. It recalls the decorations by Giulio Romano of the Palazzo del Te, Mantua, which Battista Franco may have seen.*

other dimensions. A cross-section of the house would look like the cliff-face caves of Santorin. All have curved ceilings, but curved in different ways, now barrel-vaulted, now coved, now flattened towards the centre, now semi-domed, and all are painted, so that one moves from room to room as if from one casket to another. They were designed as shapes, not for special functions. A room used as a bedroom today could become a library tomorrow; a study could be a bathroom. The wonder of it is that the whole complex, so simple in effect, so elaborately composed, is fitted together without strain or impediment.

The Villa Foscari is a house of great distinction and originality. It is fortunate that it came into the hands of such a man as Bertie Landsberg, by birth a Brazilian, before it crumbled irreparably. He died in 1965 and it now belongs to his widow. He devoted a large part of his life to its rescue. But even in the state in which he found it – whitewashed, almost windowless, one outer stairway broken away, and with only one surviving inside door – there was enough to suggest what it had been and could be again. One test of sublimity in architecture is that nothing except extreme ruin can obliterate its lines. This is true of all Palladio's work. Mr Landsberg himself best summed up its qualities in three pairs of apparent opposites; elegance and solidity; spaciousness and compactness; simplicity and grandeur.

OPPOSITE *A bedroom opening off the hall contains a fresco by Zellotti which is by tradition a portrait of one of the Foscari ladies who disgraced herself in Venice and was confined to the villa for several years. Hence 'Malcontenta'. But the legend is probably false, since the name had been attached to the land since the 13th century, perhaps because 'malcontenti', such as outlaws and escaped prisoners, took refuge here.* BELOW *The dining-room on the ground-floor is paved, vaulted and furnished with a simplicity that suits perfectly the patrician character of the whole house.*

Borreby *Zealand Denmark c.1550*

ABOVE *Big strong bricks, with granite added here and there, form the central keep of Borreby. It is still mediaeval, but there are touches which reveal the influence of the Renaissance on mid 16th-century Denmark.* TOP *Borreby is withdrawn only a few hundred yards from salt water, lying near an inlet of the island-studded strait between the Baltic and the North Sea. Originally built for defence against sea and land attack, with a sheltered harbour close by, it is today the centre of a great agricultural estate.*

OPPOSITE '*The way from the outer to the inner court is through a brick archway with whitened vaulting above, brick benches along each side and cobbles underfoot – a combination of textures, colours and shapes which immediately wins the visitor's heart. A Venetian well-head . . . makes a lovely centre-piece for the courtyard beyond.*'

The Renaissance took a long time to penetrate Denmark, and when it came it was not at first-hand from Italy, but through Holland. The main building at Borreby is dated 1556, and it was built for the leading Danish statesman of the day, Johan Friis, Chancellor to King Christian III. If ever there was an opportunity for architectural experiment, it was here, but it was an opportunity missed. The house is still basically a Gothic building, and one searches in vain for any classical detail to mark its date. But although it is bold and strong and obviously built for defence, a fumbling for new domestic forms is also evident. Thus at third-floor level a belt of stone machicolations rings the house through which scalding liquids could be poured on an aggressor; below it, between the first and second floors, the pattern is repeated by a weaker line of wavy brickwork, solely decorative in purpose. Again, the house is surrounded by a double moat, and its towers project to cover every possible approach; but the windows are large, even on the lower floors, and it could not have withstood a siege by artillery. The building is therefore a compromise between house and castle, adequate for protecting the family in civil war (the peasant rebellion in Jutland in 1536 was still a lively memory), but reflecting something of the new gracefulness arriving from Holland. The 'basket-handle' arches above the windows illustrate the architectural tremors of the times just as the different types of window illustrate the political uncertainties.

Borreby is built almost entirely of brick. Its footings are of the only two kinds of stone available in Denmark, surface boulders which were used untrimmed at foundation level, and above them big squared blocks of granite which were, presumably, brought by sea from the island of Bornholm. The main walls rest directly on the granite and are composed of straight courses of a pink brick larger in size than was used at any later date. It wears well – rather too well, for the rawness of these big bricks is partly

BELOW *The entrance, now so peaceful with its lawns, water and dripping trees, was ingeniously designed as a deterrent to marauders. Borreby is approached sideways over a wide moat, its roadway passing under a fortified gatehouse and covered by the three towers. The main house lies on an island created by a grid of moats, which are extended to include parts of the garden and farmyard.* OPPOSITE *The house in winter, from a late 18th-century painting preserved at Borreby. Since then (and indeed since the original building) there have been few external changes of any importance. The main house is in the centre, with the entrance and farmbuildings on the right, and on the left is the courtyard formed by two wings added in 1606.*

responsible for the crudity of the external appearance of the whole central building. The more delicate bricks (smaller, and more variegated in colour) used for the two buildings flanking the courtyard, which were added by Kristian Friis, Johan's nephew, in 1606, exaggerate the ungainliness of the main block. But clearly the architect, though insensitive to colour and texture, was well aware of the importance of variety. There is a great deal of buttressing and recession, giving a balance to the house and producing different shadows from different angles at different hours of the day. Seen in isolation, the central building is sturdy rather than graceful.

But no part of Borreby should be seen in isolation. The point of the house is that it is, and always was, the home of a community. It is not, like Castle Fraser, the lord's tower-house and nothing else. The central building is merely the keep of a very considerable complex of other buildings and courtyards, divided and united by moats, bridges and archways. It is from them that Borreby gains its fascination and charm. The moat surrounds the keep, but it also reaches out to embrace a large tree-lined lawn (originally the kitchen-garden) on one side and a farm-yard on the other. It is bridged by five different forms of bridge or causeway, and the garden extends beyond the moat, providing raised walks and shaded lawns all round the house. Thus is the keep softened by grass, trees and water. But it is also softened by the other buildings, which are built less aggressively and with greater sympathy for the materials. For example, the way from the outer to the inner court is through a brick archway with whitened vaulting above, brick benches along each side and cobbles underfoot – a combination of textures, colours and shapes which immediately wins the visitor's heart. A Venetian well-head of the same date as the main house, but wholly different in feeling, makes a lovely centre-piece for the courtyard beyond.

Borreby was never attacked, but it was well equipped to resist attack if it came. There was but one entrance to the main building, located in the tower on the south side, and this could

only be approached by crossing a draw-bridge. The upper floor of the keep was in effect a fighting floor. From it every approach could be deluged with fire through loop-holes pierced in the brickwork. The living quarters were on the ground-floor above a high basement, while the big hall, still used for festive occasions, was on the floor above. The floors are joined by a turret staircase, which, internally, is the loveliest part of the keep, for the bricks have paradoxically mellowed better inside than outside, and the square or spiral flights are composed of worn stone treads taken from a neighbouring monastery, dissolved in the Danish Reformation of 1536. The rooms have very frequently been re-shaped and redecorated since Renaissance times. One of them retains its original painted rafters, and the 18th-century drawing-room shows how fine a house could be contrived within a fortress. The three turrets on the north side provide smaller rooms on each floor, some of them, including the little library, attractively vaulted. Some make bedrooms; others bathrooms. The whole house is capable of frequent adaptation to changing needs, and is today a perfect setting for tapestries and antique furniture.

The Friis family held Borreby until 1618 when it passed into the hands of the Daas. Valdemar Daa is best remembered for Hans Andersen's narrative of the sad fate which overtook him. Having dabbled in alchemy to restore his family's fortunes, he then invested in the construction of a ship for the King's navy, but the King would not purchase the ship without Daa's fine black horses which he refused to sell with it. The ship remained unsold, and Borreby was forfeited to its mortgagee, Ove Ramel. The manor passed through various other hands, until in 1783 it was bought by Major General Sir Melchior Holten Castenschiold, in whose family it still remains. Indeed, four generations now live in different parts of the house. Adolf Frederik Holten Castenschiold, who inherited the property in 1919, lives in the keep; his son in the chapel wing; his grandson and great-grandchildren in the wing opposite. In the outer courtyards and surrounding estate-cottages live a dozen other families dependent for their livelihood on this thriving manor-farm. Borreby is constructed on a big scale, and it radiates an atmosphere of goodwill.

ABOVE *The chapel in the West wing was altered to its present appearance by the family of Berregaard, who were the owners of Borreby in the mid 18th century. Among their additions was this charming 'font', still used for christenings. An angel, swinging by a metal rod from the ceiling, holds a silver dish.* ABOVE LEFT *The large hall, or Riddersal, of Borreby on its first floor. The main living-quarters were below and the 'fighting-floor', with loop-holed windows, above. This great room was only used on festive occasions, and still is; and although it has been restored in modern times, it is evident how comfortable a house could be made within a formidable keep.* OPPOSITE *The interior of the main staircase, contained within the central turret of the keep. The stone treads were taken from a neighbouring monastery demolished during the Danish Reformation of 1536. The defensive nature of the embrasures is very apparent, and here the big bricks with their fine colour come into their own.*

Villa Lante *Bagnaia Italy 1556-89*

Anyone who is weary of stupendous houses posing as palaces; anyone who seeks in Italy the more tender aspects of the Renaissance; anyone who believes erroneously that humanism means a divorce between man and nature; anyone, in short, who wishes to know what the Italians of the 16th century contributed to the art of living, and why it is that their influence is still felt today, should visit the Villa Lante at Bagnaia, three miles from Viterbo. The place is an enchantment. One speaks of an Italian villa, and the picture conjured up is of a pink or yellow building with a rippled roof, set on a minor hilltop with an avenue of cypresses marking its approach. What matters is the view of it, and the view from it. The Villa Lante is quite different from this, and yet it is obviously Italian. There is no single house; there are twin pavilions set side by side, unconnected even by a subterranean passage, so that for a moment one wonders where, or which, the villa can be. Perhaps these are entrance lodges? Perhaps the main house lies in the woods behind? Perhaps one of the pavilions was intended for the family, and the other for the servants? But no. The Villa Lante is divided into two identical blocks, with the garden in front of, between, behind and around them, and the only distinction which one can hazard is that the right-hand pavilion was normally occupied by the owners and the left-hand pavilion by their guests.

There is certainly a view from it, over the roof-tops of Bagnaia, but there is no view of it except by peering through the bars of the gate at its entrance. It lies not on a hilltop, but halfway down a long slope which is continued beyond the gate by the village street. Yet it is not hidden, nor disdainfully withdrawn from village life. Although it expresses the utmost in refinement and aristocratic living, it is still of the country and of the people, and it comes as no surprise to learn that it was built between 1546 and 1578 ('created' is the apter word) by a Cardinal-Archbishop of Viterbo, who loved it beyond all his other worldly possessions, and appears to have been a simple though learned man, who wished to escape his episcopal cares in a country retreat where

Few houses, and even fewer gardens, can have been altered so little since their conception. This view of the Villa Lante by Pannini (LEFT) made in the early 18th century, is almost identical with the same scene today. The Fountain of the Moors lies in the centre of the Quadrato below the two parts of the villa.

elaboration was made to appear modest, and extravagance unassuming. The division of the house into two separate parts is one example of this. Another is the marriage between house and garden, conceived almost for the first time as a single unit, instead of making one the adjunct of the other. And a third, the use of trees and water as the main elements in the composition, linking house and garden to the countryside, just as if nature had done most, and man least.

The effect is therefore rural, companionable. There is an element of expectation, for the layout is symmetrical and both parts of the villa and the shape of the garden can be clearly seen from almost any point in it ; but there is also an element of surprise, for its main effects are held in reserve until you come suddenly upon them, and an exploration of the garden is like the exploration of a well-planned exhibition. Its purpose is immediately apparent; but many of its delights are on an intimate scale, and amuse the visitor by their ingenuity and novelty, while preserving a sense of decorum and calm. The Villa Lante contains jokes, like sprays of water which would suddenly drench an unsuspecting visitor, and there is a faint note of comedy throughout. This, perhaps, is the secret of the place : there is comedy, but not ribaldry ; seclusion, but it is not a hermitage ; ingenuity, but it is not a box of tricks ; romance, and yet parts of it are severe. We see it today lovelier than its creators saw it, for the stones have mellowed, and the trees grown high. Yet in imagination the Cardinals must have envisaged these effects of centuries, and foreseen that leaves and moss and the natural wearing of stone by water would soften the place, render it more private and serene. In the interval taste has not changed to the extent that we are puzzled by their motives or find their innovations absurd. Indeed, just like a discovery in science, the villa was a discovery in the combination of natural and artificial elements which has added something of permanent **value to mankind. It still makes sense; it still gives pleasure** If you were asked to take, say, a Chinaman, or an African, to one place in Europe which would sum up what Europe has contributed to the arts, you could do no better than take him to the Villa Lante.

The key to the villa, its liquid core, is water. Water not for drinking or floating or cleansing, but water as a sound, as a reflector of light, as a diversion. It comes from natural springs in the surrounding hills, and thence is led by aqueducts to a reservoir (which also acted as a fishpond for the Cardinal's table) in the upper part of the park. From here it is conducted underground to a waterfall at the very top of the garden. This is the beginning of the chain of fountains and hydraulic novelties which descend through the garden, between the two pavilions, to the largest of the fountains in the centre of the *parterre*, and thence, again underground, to a fountain in the middle of the village. It falls by gravity, since the slope is steep, and there is not a pump needed in the whole arrangement to force the water through the dozen fountains, and it flows on day and night, year after year, under its natural momentum. Ideally, one should follow the water downhill, but the main garden, the *Quadrato*, lies towards the bottom alongside the entrance, and the ascent of the five terraces takes one against the current, which seems to be against the laws of nature. There is, however, a path leading through the park, beside one of the most dramatic of the fountains, the Fountain of Pegasus, by which the top can be reached without going through the garden itself, and this is by far the best approach.

The water comes from the hillside, overgrown with bushes, and falls in light beards against an artificial rock background. This primeval beginning was, of course, quite deliberate. Humanism required that the control of the natural elements by man be demonstrated, and as the cascades descend from platform to platform the formality becomes more and more pronounced. The symbolism is perhaps lost on us today, and what entrances us is the variety of the descent, the different combinations of wet stone and dry stone, of sculpture and hydraulics, of dripping water and dripping trees, and always the sound of the prattling stream eagerly feeding onwards to meet an unknown fate just below – where it may be required to slide along a long sloping trough, the *catena d'acqua*, which is now waisted to increase the pressure, now opens out into shallow brackets, or to issue from the mouth of a mask or a lion, or to flow between urns along a balustrade, or along the central channel of a stone table where the Cardinal served his guests *al fresco* banquets (using the water to cool the wine), or to be split up into a score of little jets set like candles round an altar. The water is thus often suspended on stone at the level of a lowered hand, tamed momentarily, and then released to resume its natural fall; and often it is shaped by the construction of the jets into flames, fans, or the parabola of an arrow's flight, as well as tumbling loose, thick and urgent when it is gathered back into a single outpouring. Two great river-gods of stone, the Tiber and the Arno, recline below one of the fountains, indifferent to the impertinent ripple of the water between them, and indifferent to each other, for their heads are turned away as if refusing in perpetuity to be introduced. Elsewhere, above the Pegasus fountain, the herms gaze down benignly upon the prancing horse, engaged in a murmur of conversation rendered inaudible by the falling water. And sometimes we find a statue for-

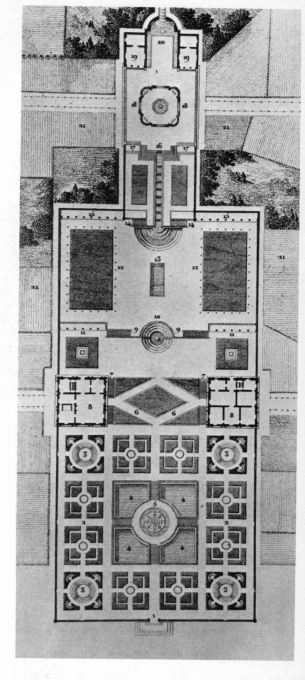

ABOVE *A plan of the garden at the Villa Lante made in Paris in 1809. The twin pavilions are both numbered 8. The rest of the plan shows the position of the various gardens and fountains. The water enters at the top (No 20) and flows by gravity to the Fountain of the Moors (No 5) and then underground to the village below the gate (No 1).*

OPPOSITE *Inside the loggia of the right-hand pavilion, showing on the end wall a perspective view of the completed layout of the Villa Lante made before the second pavilion had even been begun.*

ever alone in a grotto, wet and a bit sad, resenting the indignity of being turned into a fountain, for there is a limited number of orifices in the human body from which water can be emitted without either absurdity or offence. Picture, too, alongside all this glorious tumbling and spurting, a canopy of ilexes and plane trees, and solemn rows of fluted columns or stone jars, and branching steps by which it is a joy to descend, for alternative balustraded steps are always presented to right or left, leading to flat ground at last, at the villa's heart, the Fountain of the Moors.

They are called Moors because their stone skins are so blackened by the water as to be almost indistinguishable from bronze, but they are idealised youths of the Roman Renaissance, superbly unconscious of their nakedness, holding aloft the arms of the Montalto family, humps surmounted by a star from the points of which water spurts like shafts of light. Between their feet crouch two pairs of lions. Around this central feature is a rectangular basin crossed by flat bridges, with stone boats in the waterfilled quadrants, each occupied by a musketeer whose musket is given the appearance of a fishing-rod by the curving jet of water that comes from it. And beyond again lies the great *parterre*, divided by low yews or lower box-hedging, as neat and ingeniously scrolled as the loops of a model railway.

At this point, one remembers that the Villa Lante is a house as well as a garden. The second (left-hand) pavilion was completed in 1589 after some ten years had elapsed since the building of the first, and in the interval the property had passed from Cardinal Gian Francesco Gambara, the real creator of the Villa Lante and its garden, to Cardinal Montalto, a grand-nephew of Pope Sixtus V. But both pavilions were planned from the very beginning, as is shown in the fresco of the whole *ensemble* painted in the

loggia of the first pavilion before the second was begun. The design is attributed to Vignola, the architect of the neighbouring Palazzo Farnese at Caprarola. There are many points in common between the gardens of the two houses, but the houses themselves could not be more different: the one stupendous, arrogant, fortress-like; the other intimate, charming and reserved. Flat pilasters and alternating rounded and rectilinear pediments to the windows were all that Vignola would allow himself as decoration on the exterior walls of the Villa Lante, and neat belvederes on the roofs. Inside, there is greater freedom. All the ceilings and many of the walls are frescoed, and there is much variety in the arrangement of the rooms in the two pavilions, the 'Montalto' pavilion containing the largest room, and the other a nest of small *stanze* on three floors, which are perfectly adapted for occupation for two or three weeks at a time. The villa was not a permanent residence, but the Cardinal-Bishop's summer-house, and magnificence would have been out of place and out of scale.

Today the villa belongs to the *Società Villa Lante*, and has been restored under the direction of Dr Angelo Cantoni to its original appearance. Both house and garden are in perfect condition. Is it a 'great house' in the context of this volume? In size, no; in sublimity, yes. If it is accepted that a garden can be as much part of a house as its loggias or the landscapes painted in lunettes on its walls, then the Villa Lante can take its place without inferiority alongside the noblest edifices that men have created for their habitation.

FAR LEFT *The craw-fish or* gambero *of the Cardinal's arms on the casino at the top of the garden.*

BELOW *Part of the cornice of the* Salone di Conversazione *in the left-hand, or Montalto, pavilion, which was probably reserved for the Cardinal's guests.*

CARRO · DI · GIVN

CARRO · DI · CERERE

In the period of Scottish architecture contemporary with the first English Queen Elizabeth, lairds enlarged their houses by adding towers to them, without much caring whether the result was symmetrical so long as it was strong. Then in the early 17th century, they began to build lengthwise instead of upwards. The two periods are illustrated BELOW. *The keep, with its added towers, dates substantially from 1550-1600 ; the two long wings, of which one is here visible, were completed by Andrew Fraser in 1636.* OPPOSITE *The turret-tops, and even the dormer windows, could be French, but not the heavy moulding on which they rest. The influence is that of mediaeval Scottish castles, not of the French Renaissance, although the turrets were by this time decorative and useful, not defensive. They look splendid from a distance, and form interesting annexes to the rooms inside.*

Castle Fraser

Aberdeenshire Scotland c.1570-1636

The best moment to see Castle Fraser for the first time is in the evening of a summer's day. You catch sight of it across an open park of a verdant trimness which one associates more with England than Scotland, half-hidden by the trees but gleaming palely between them, its major towers repeating the rotundity of their trunks and its upperworks their crowns. The house lies low in a shallow valley, rising clifflike from grass and gravel, with nothing, not even a garden, to distract the eye from its original period and lines. Sharp it is, with its poignard turret-tops, but its rounded towers swell like lighthouses, and it stands firmly self-contained, a mixture of architectural sexes, masculine as far as the roofline, feminine above, a page torn from an illuminated Book of Hours. It is stubbornly defensive, yet contains no hint of menace. A secret place ; a haunted place. Its walls, where exposed, are as rough as stone just taken from the moor, but careful craftmanship is evident in the survival of even its most delicate parts.

A castle ? Yes, in more than name, for it was built to resist intrusion if not attack, and many of its features are derived from the keeps of mediaeval Scotland. But it is a house, too, since as the towers mount upwards they bifurcate into turrets and dormer windows, promising comfort and seclusion within, and on the north side two companionable wings enclose a courtyard by which the visitor feels welcomed and drawn in. To this unique product of Scottish architecture the name 'tower-house' is usually given. It is a good one, since it suggests both the history of this type of building and that combination of austerity and high spirits which were so characteristic of the age. We call it romantic, because its turrets, its apparent lack of symmetry, its hard thick walls and the surprise of coming upon something so Gothic in the

middle of radiant countryside make it seem far older than it is, representative of an age and attitudes as remote from our own as the true castles of the robber-barons of the Western Isles. We expect, half hope, to find it a ruin. When we discover it to be intact, in part inhabited and wholly inhabitable, we are anxious to discover why men chose to build like this only three-and-a-half centuries ago, and to analyse its weird perfection.

Nobody could deny the builders of Castle Fraser a sense of proportion. When you consider how the arrangement and decoration of a normal house have here been reversed, with the most glorious effects reserved for the upper storeys, it is surprising that it does not seem top-heavy or absurd. How has its balance been achieved? By much the same methods as a man-of-war. The poops, masts and gun-turrets spring from its upperworks, while the carcass is strong and slim. Although there is immense variety in its silhouette (therefore it can be viewed from every direction with equal pleasure), the scale of its vertical projections is in perfect harmony with the mass of its supporting towers. The skyline of an ordinary house is more often than not a cluster of chimneys which the eye accepts as a domestic necessity, as one day, by force of habit, it may come to accept a thicket of television aerials. But at Castle Fraser the chimneys are quite unobtrusive, and we have in their place tall conical or ogival caps rising to about the same height as chimneys, but by their shape, size and disposition infinitely more satisfying and suggestive. Horizontally as well as vertically the façades of the house combine solidity with surprise. There are frequent re-entrants where one tower joins another at right-angles or on a curve; a strong belt of carved stone at two-thirds of the height, as pronounced as the embroidered neckline to a shirt; a grouping of ringed corbels to support the turrets; and rows of windows disposed symmetrically to relieve, but not

TOP *'Fraser does not have the closed look of a castle, but the frank look of a house.' This is mainly because it has large windows, some quite close to the ground. Another reason is the obvious interest taken in external decoration; and a third, the variation between rough walls and smooth.* ABOVE *Some of the stones forming the main walls seem barely to have been shaped, but the masonry, where it mattered, was superb. The little object in the centre is not a gargoyle, a water-pipe or a cannon, but a purely decorative projection pretending to be all three.* OPPOSITE *The roofs from one of the higher towers. This is the side of the castle away from the main entrance, where two wings were added in the early 17th century. One of them can be seen extending towards the park and forming one side of a service courtyard at the back.*

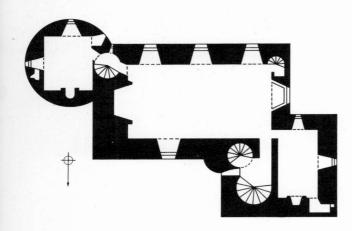

TOP *The spiral staircase leading out of the chapel at Castle Fraser.* ABOVE *The ground-plan of the first floor of the main block illustrates not only the starkness and sturdiness of the structure, but the difficulty of finding your way to the hall, the large room in the centre. Access was deliberately designed to be by spiral staircases up opposite towers, in order to make attack more difficult, and escape easier.* OPPOSITE *When the work on the main block was completed, the date 1618 was added above a window; but in the previous year this magnificent heraldic table was mounted on the courtyard side of the house, incorporating the royal arms of England and Scotland, and modestly below, '1617. I.BEL. M.M.F.', thought to be the signature of the Master Mason to Fraser.*

weaken, the massiveness of the keep. The colour of the walls is pinky-grey where they are 'harled' (covered with a weatherproof rendering of lime and sand), and rough in texture, like porridge, when they are not. Against them gently stir the shadows of the surrounding trees.

The temptation to seek a French influence in the architecture of Castle Fraser must be resisted. Certainly there was a strong cultural link between France and Scotland, and French masons are known to have worked on the royal palaces of this period. But the builders of the house, the Frasers of the late 16th and early 17th centuries, had no close connections with France, and its master-mason is known to have been I. Bell, a member of a well-known family of local craftsmen. Besides, only the turret-tops are superficially French. Where in France would you find squat roundels hanging like wasp-nests from the eaves, or such blankness of the lower walls, or the stepped string-course which wanders between and under the corbelling of the turrets? It is simpler to search for the origin of these tower-houses in Scotland itself, for in all parts of the country, in ruin or in perfect preservation, one can see examples of their antecedents, and follow the slow adaptation of ancient forms of fortification to the demand for greater comfort and convenience. Sometimes, as at Huntly Castle, also in Aberdeenshire, one can see all phases of construction and reconstruction, from the 12th century to the 17th, in a single group. Internal partition-walls multiply; towers are thrown out from the main keep for defence and to provide private rooms leading off the hall; dormer-windows advance from behind the parapet flush with the outer walls; battlements become balustrades and wall-top defences ornamental turrets. All these developments are well documented in stone. Castle Fraser is the direct descendant of the 13th-century keep.

What is surprising is that the Scottish nobility of the period immediately following the union of the two Crowns did not abandon their ancestral tradition more completely. After all, they were not untravelled ignoramuses. They had in the palaces of Stirling, Linlithgow, Holyroodhouse and Falkland superb examples of the new 'horizontal' style of building, which did not require the ladies of the house always to be ascending and descending tight spiral staircases between sweating walls, nor the laird to dine in the same hall where his henchmen slept. Their fidelity to the tower-house is ascribed to sentiment, to the shortage of brick and timber (the roof-beams for the wings at Castle Fraser had to be imported from Norway), to the desire to impress by sheer height, and to the needs of defence. This last explanation is not wholly convincing. Although the walls were six to nine feet thick at the base and pitted with holes for muskets, the tower-house was utterly defenceless against artillery, and there were no protective outworks, not even a moat or a ditch. Its situation cannot have been chosen by anyone who wished to keep the surrounding country under constant watch. The lower walls are bare, but not windowless. Those in the round tower extend almost to the ground, and the four great windows of the hall on the first floor appear to be original, though they may have been en-

That it was possible to live comfortably on the upper storeys of this great tower-house is indicated by the two photographs on this page, one of the mistress's bedroom and one of a sitting-room, both retaining their 19th-century decorations and furnishings. But there is still no running water in the house, and no electric light in the majority of the rooms. OPPOSITE *'The interior reveals better than the outside the 16th-century Frasers' reluctance to break with the past . . . There is a monastic severity about the hall . . . The granite expressed and imposed a Spartan way of life.' It was the main room of the house for many generations. The portrait of General Alexander Mackenzie Fraser, who commanded one of the British divisions at the battle of Corunna, hangs above the fireplace.*

larged. Fraser does not have the closed look of a castle, but the frank look of a house.

One additional reason why Castle Fraser was built like this, as one of the last and certainly one of the greatest of the tower-houses, is that its roots may already have been there. Archaeologists are still disputing whether the building incorporates work earlier than the mid-16th century, but the most authoritative of them all, Dr W. Douglas Simpson, thinks that it does not. What is certain is that the square tower known as Michael Tower, after its builder Michael Fraser, cannot be later than 1576, for a carved stone bears that date, and it may have been erected even earlier as a hunting-lodge. The main block and the circular tower, diagonally opposite Michael Tower, were added in about 1600 in the same general style, following the tradition that you enlarged your house by adding towers. Then, some fifteen years later, the whole building was heightened and transformed by Michael's son, Andrew, who retained the lower structure as far as the fretted band and added above it the whole complicated panoply of turrets, dormers and the steeply pitched roof. The dormers bear the date of completion, 1618. The wings were added, also by Andrew, in 1621-36. Thus the minimum period of building extends over sixty years, and during that time the tastes and habits of the lairds had changed considerably. The lower and older parts of the castle are still mediaeval in spirit; the upper parts and wings reflect the greater stability of the times, and the influence, though much diluted, of the Renaissance. The Frasers telescoped into sixty years what English architects had taken three hundred to evolve, because the English started earlier. But it should be remembered that Castle Fraser is contemporary with such English houses as Knole and Blickling, and even (in its

LEFT *The front-door was inserted in the early 19th century, at the same time as the windows above it may have been enlarged. The coats-of-arms were brought from other parts of the building, after the habit of the Scots for rearranging their family escutcheons like stamp-collections.* BELOW *The courtyard side of the house was added early in the 17th century, with the same architectural feeling, reminiscent of France, but with a greater concern for domesticity. Part of the walled garden is beyond on the right.*

last and most dramatic phase) with Inigo Jones's Wilton. There
was still a very wide gap.

The interior reveals better than the outside the 16th-century
Frasers' reluctance to break with the past. The room at the base
of the round tower is dungeon-like in its dim rotundity, though it
was probably never used for anything but storage, while the
kitchens on the ground floor are more like cellars than rooms,
mere cavities in the vast foundations, but whitened and well-lit,
with walls, ceilings and fireplaces bowed with the strain of supporting so great a bulk. On the floor above is the main suite – the
hall, and a withdrawing room in each tower. The ceilings are
barrel-vaulted. There is a monastic severity about the hall, from
the huge fireplace at one end to the stone window-seat at the
other. The granite expressed and imposed a Spartan way of life.
Of course, it was not necessarily always so gaunt as it appears
today. One must in imagination add the colours of tapestry,
silver, heraldic shields and jewelled clothes. In the near-contem-
porary Aberdeenshire tower-houses of Crathes, Midmar and
Craigievar one can still see panelling, wall-painting and plasterwork of which Castle Fraser must surely once have had its share.
But its interior can never have been so splendid as theirs, for later
owners would have been at pains to preserve whatever 17th-
century decorations they found, as they so faithfully preserved
the outside. There are other features about Castle Fraser which
slightly chill the blood. A chamber concealed in the groin of the
hall's vaulting, and approachable only through a trapdoor in the
laird's bedroom above, enabled him to overhear every word
spoken in the window-seat of the hall. There is a similar eaves-
dropping chamber at Speke Hall in Lancashire, but it dates from
a hundred years earlier. Again the Scottish timelag in morals and
manners! In all parts of the house one finds spy-holes and gun-
loops, traps for the treacherous and unwary, and, not surprisingly,
a ghost, bloodstained steps and inexplicable sounds after dark.

The last of the male Frasers of that line, Charles Fraser the
Younger of Castle Fraser, was killed in 1746, fighting for the
Young Pretender at Culloden, and the property passed to his
maiden sister, Elyza Fraser, who held it until 1814. She made
various improvements to the house, including a new front door on
the south front, not ill-suited to its old walls, and a timber staircase, since removed, to supplement the spiral stairs which still
make access to the upper floors so perplexing to a stranger. It was
she, and her immediate successors, who partitioned and redecorated the loftier part of the house, and so radically altered its
arrangements that it is now almost impossible to recover the 17th-
century plan. Their improvements made the house habitable
without disturbing its elevations, which remain Castle Fraser's
chief glory. But except for flats in the two wings, it is not now
occupied. The present owners, Major and Mrs Michael Smiley,
live in the delightful 18th-century stable-hexagon a few hundred
yards across the park. From its entrance archway one sees the
castle towering above the trees, a gilded weathercock glinting
from almost a hundred feet up, above a battery of gargoyles
pretending to be guns.

*'A gilded weathercock glinting from almost a hundred
feet up.' On the right, across a short stretch of the park,
can be seen part of the 18th-century stables, which the
present owners of the Castle Fraser have converted into
a house for themselves.*

Schloss Langenburg *Württemberg Germany 1580-1616*

The countryside in what has been known for centuries as 'the Hohenloher Land' is the picture of Germany which most non-Germans retain in their minds. It is called a plain because it rises to no peaks; but it is split by deep river-valleys which create swirling contours below the general level, and into them dip woods and meadows and sturdy red-roofed villages. One such valley is that of the River Jagst. The town of Langenburg lies on a tongue of land which forces the river to describe a tight loop around its base, and on the very tip of the tongue is the castle. From it, on three sides, the ground falls away to the river. Until little more than a hundred years ago the steep slopes were vine-covered; now they are forested. The castle's walls and towers rise firmly from a bed of leaves, continuing on a grander scale the line of houses forming the town.

12th-century or 20th-century? Incredibly, both; and much in between. Nothing is more surprising about this enchanting place than to find on the apex of the gable facing the town the date 1966. During the night of 24 January 1963 fire destroyed one and a half wings of the castle, including the block where the family lived. It was a night of bitter cold. The roads were icy, the hydrants frozen and the nearest full-sized fire-brigade was three hours away at Stuttgart. It seemed impossible that any part of the castle could be saved. When they attempted to pump up water from the river 500 feet below, it froze in the hoses half-way. In the end they made a chain of artificial reservoirs up the slope, and by this means created a sufficient pressure of water to reach the highest point of the blaze. So intense was the cold that the water turned to ice on the still smoking beams, and the added weight brought them crashing down. By morning the east end of the castle was a shell. Those of the walls which still stood were bowed

OPPOSITE *The River Jagst lies hidden at the foot of the tree-covered slopes. Once they were planted with vines, as shown ABOVE in a painting made in 1699 of Graf von Hohenlohe-Langenburg with his family. Both views are from approximately the same spot, and almost no change is apparent in the profile of the house after the passage of nearly three hundred years. The earliest part of the building, lying on the left, dates from about 1150, and the round towers on the right were added about a century later. The gabled wing between them, and the tall lookout tower, are late 16th century.*

outwards by the stresses of the fire, and when the damage was first surveyed, it seemed probable that they would have to be rebuilt from ground level. Later a method was found of pinning and strengthening the walls, and with the aid of photographs the original external appearance of the castle was reconstructed, and the opportunity taken to make considerable internal changes to the layout of the rooms occupied by the family.

The most historic part of Langenburg was saved—its round angle towers, and the greater part of its famous courtyard. What was destroyed, and is now rebuilt, is the east end of the courtyard which had been largely reconstructed once before, in the mid-18th century. The fire, in other words, was a personal more than an architectural disaster, and Langenburg still holds its place among the loveliest and most interesting of all the German castles.

The earliest part is the west end, on the very tip of the tongue, where, in about 1150, a thick knot of towers and turrets was constructed by dependants of the Hohenstaufen emperors. This still exists, almost unchanged. About a hundred years later, when we first find the Hohenlohes associated with the place, the two towers of the east end were built and the double dry-moat dug in front of them, to cut off from the town the peninsula on which the castle stood. It was at this stage a fortress, not a house. Its only living-quarters were wooden barracks between the two groups of towers, and the Hohenlohes, living in their main castles at Weikersheim, Ohringen and Neuenstein, would have put Langenburg under the command of a local captain. In 1234 it withstood its first siege.

This mediaeval part of Langenburg is equally impressive from inside or out. The masonry is on a cyclopean scale, the outward faces of the huge blocks of stone being left in the rough except for smoothed strips where the blocks lay against each other, and the dungeon-like walls, in places 12 feet thick, rise unshakeably from the rock, massively rotund and arched, vaulted below and pinnacled above, the very picture of mediaeval pride and independence. Today a circuit-walk has been contrived through the woods at the base of the wall, and it is a dramatic experience to pick one's way round the curves of the great drum-towers and between the trees. But to sense to the full the impressive construction of these fortifications, one must see them from inside, looking down from an internal doorway halfway up a tower upon the straw-strewn circle of its floor, lit by a deep wedge of golden light streaming through an arrow-slit.

It was in the 1580s that Langenburg began to acquire its present appearance. In that decade Graf Wolfgang von Hohenlohe started the construction of high permanent wings to join the two groups of towers, creating between them a courtyard house of very considerable size. As he simultaneously began to build even more ambitiously at Weikersheim, the work at Langenburg was interrupted after the north side of the courtyard had been completed, and it was only resumed under Philip Ernst Hohenlohe some thirty years later. An inscription running round two sides of the courtyard records that it was finished by him in six years, 1610–16, right up to the turret-tops.

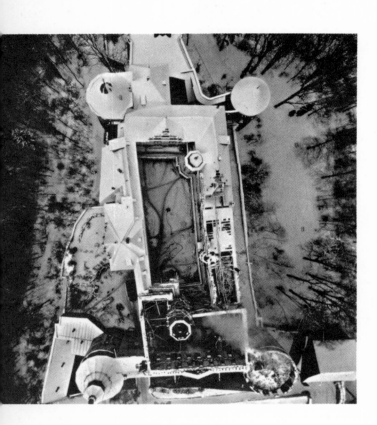

This astonishing photograph of Langenburg was taken vertically from the air soon after the fire of 24 January 1963. The embers are still smouldering. The large areas of white on the roofs are due not to overexposure of the film, but to snow. Three of the four mediaeval angle-towers survived intact, but the east end and north-east corner of the courtyard were gutted and have since been rebuilt.

The entrance façade, almost all of which was restored from drawings and photographs exactly as it was before the fire of 1963. The date 1966 is inscribed in the gable. The only part of the original building seen here is the drum-tower on the left, which contains the chapel. The slopes of the hill-spur on which the castle stands are too steep for gardening, so the garden lies outside, beside the causeway leading across the moat to the castle-entrance.

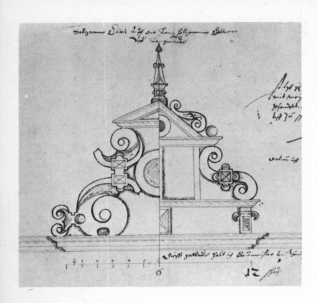

This courtyard is still Gothic in feeling, although here and there classical motifs have been introduced, such as the Ionic and Corinthian capitals to the columns supporting the two galleries on the south side. There is also an attempt at symmetry in the placing of the three gables of the opposite wing. But the cheerful, haphazard inventiveness of the mediaeval builders keeps breaking in to confound the good intentions of the 'Renaissance' style. As there were no communicating doors from room to room on the first floor, an external gallery was built to link them, and this gallery was carried round the entire circuit of the courtyard, corbelled out from the walls on huge twirly brackets and edged with a parapet of scrolled stone. Again, as there were no internal staircases, the stairs were spiralled up towers built where convenience but not symmetry demanded. These towers, in turn, interrupted the gallery, which was either carried round them or driven through them by arches. An entrance to the courtyard had to be made, and a lookout tower built to survey the country and provide an impressive centre-piece when the castle was viewed from outside. When all these elements had been fitted in, the 'Renaissance' courtyard had become a jumble. But what a delightful jumble! The building is solid enough – too solid it would have seemed, with its heavy over-insurance of supporting stone, until the fire proved its value – but there are touches of fancy and even delicacy, as in the three superimposed galleries of fretted stone on the east side, subtly shortening as they mount, or the combination of horizontal and vertical elements at the same end.

Whether the effect is due to design or accident is difficult to say; certainly self-conscious charm would have ruined it. This courtyard has come together by the fusion of different needs, among which we must count the need for security, the need for comfort, and the need for a certain amount of dignified display, for Langenburg was then the centre of a little kingdom of twelve villages. The courtyard was the womb of the house. After all the outward looking, there must be some inward looking too. One must imagine this place filled with sounds and smells and stolen glimpses – of horses clattering over the drawbridge, of maid-servants calling to each other across, or up, or down, of much washing and scouring, of the rolling-in of barrels, of fluttering handkerchiefs and disappearing petticoats and little lamps; of assemblies, too, of men-at-arms or tenantry or troupes of players and musicians; even, one likes to imagine, of tourneys and other warlike games.

Dominating the whole is the tall tower, still capped by the lion of Langenburg bearing the metal standard pierced with the letters PEHL (Philip Ernst Hohenlohe-Langenburg) and the date 1616. When in 1757 Graf Ludwig Hohenlohe rebuilt this end, the tower was heightened to rise above the heightened roof and the lion re-erected at a greater eminence; but the corbels of the original parapet were left ringing the tower and now emerge like wheel-spokes around it – a happy, unconventional tribute by a later age to an earlier. Otherwise this side of the court remained unchanged (and was precisely reconstructed after the fire), but on the far side, overlooking the moats and the town, a thin block of

buildings was built out in the 1760s beyond the curtain wall, providing it with a new façade in the style of provincial baroque, and the entrance was changed to pass between the two mediaeval towers over fixed bridges. This 'baroque' front forms a pleasant entrance to the house, very welcoming, very neat and convenient above the yawning moat, with a roof speckled by tiny dormer-windows, like young eager eyes seen from below, like little lids from above. Behind this white façade are the new rooms of the 1963-6 reconstruction, and behind them again is the thick wall of the 13th-century defences.

Langenburg is a house of exteriors. Its rooms have been so much altered, twisted into such odd shapes by the grafting of new on old, that not much is left to suggest how people lived here in former times. There is one excellent Renaissance ceiling of stuccoed panels – hefty bare limbs and sturdy cattle – and a long gallery of the early 17th century. A chapel was formed in 1621 from one of the entrance towers, where the confined circular shape has been adapted by building up the pews in tiered galleries, a pulpit rising in their midst—a lovely composition which Fürst Hohenlohe hopes soon to restore. There are rooms and rooms for which no more than occasional use is found. High up on the roof overlooking the courtyard is a suspended cottage (there is no better way of describing the complexity of these German gables), which could one day perhaps become a completely separate dwelling; while at ground-level there are cavernous mediaeval store-rooms, like gaps between the roots of a huge tree, in which the apparatus and weapons (there are two cannon) of many generations can gather rust and grime. Nevertheless, this is a house full of life and young affection. It has not forgotten the great fire but come to terms with it, as is only fitting for the dwelling of a family which has a phoenix as its crest.

RIGHT *One end of the 17th-century long gallery, which has excellent stucco on the ceiling. A rampant phoenix, the crest of the Hohenlohe family, stands on a bracket above the stoves.* BELOW *The present generation of Hohenlohes, who still live at Langenburg, have been careful to preserve different periods of the internal decoration. This is one of a small suite of Victorian rooms at the west end, overlooking from its windows the earliest part of the castle, dating from seven centuries earlier.*

Parham Park *Sussex England 1577-83*

Walking along the ridge of the West Sussex Downs you follow a route which men and driven animals have taken for thousands of years between the clay of the Weald and the broad shelf of the coastal plain. On one side the horizon is bounded by the iron sheet of the English Channel, and inland you look across woods, ponds, villages and the chalky lozenges of ploughed land. Midway along the ridge, you will notice below you and to the north an enclosure of some three hundred acres, set apart from its surroundings by the absence of cultivation or dividing hedges, and a mixture of large coniferous trees with beech and oak. Deer wander in this park ; swans and herons flap over it ; there is a lake ; a little church ; some thatched barns and cottages ; and, in its approximate centre, a great grey house. You can see it clearly from the Down, a mile from its foot, a stone building with a stone roof, broken in outline by gables, dormers, brick chimney-stacks, a flagpole and the white bell-tower of the stable-block behind. The sun, catching the projections of the house and its many-faceted windows, speckles it with points of light.

Something of the house or houses which stood here since before the Norman Conquest is still incorporated in the present walls. Parham was a manor which belonged to Westminster Abbey for nearly five hundred years. Cavernous fireplaces and orifices for ovens or latrines are still to be seen in the lower floors of the east wing. A Henry VII archway frames the entrance to a larder, and between the roots of the house you come across blocks of masonry of uncertain purpose but reassuring massiveness. Surviving farm-registers and legal records, including Domesday Book, supplement the evidence of these remains. But the more tangible history of Parham begins on a day and at an hour which we can identify precisely. An account-book belonging to the Verney family of Fairfield, Somerset, contains this note:

> '28 January 1577. The foundation of Parham House was first begun to be laid, and Mr Thomas Palmer laid the first stone thereof about ten of the clock in the forenoon of the same day, being then of the age of two years and a half at Christmas last.'

Sir Thomas Palmer, the boy's grandfather, had inherited the manor from his own father who bought it from the Crown in 1540

ABOVE *Parham is not of unmanageable size, but with its stable-court behind and the little church across the lawn in front, it is a lovely example of the larger English country-house. Its nationality is immediately identifiable.* OPPOSITE *The south front, which faces towards the Downs. The house was completely rebuilt in 1577, but the wing on the extreme right still incorporates part of the mediaeval building.*

The drawing above was made in 1790 by Rev. Steb-bing Shaw, and comparison between it and the photograph on the previous page makes clear where the 19th century altered the fenestration and gables. Fortunately it left untouched the most important feature of this front, the Elizabethan windows of the hall. OPPOSITE *'Ladderlike the mullioned windows climb the façades', and the greatest of them are those shown here, the windows of the hall, with (above, on the right) one of the dormer windows of the long gallery.*

after the dissolution of the Abbey lands. For thirty-three years Sir Thomas occupied the old house on his visits to Sussex before deciding at the age of nearly sixty to rebuild it. Perhaps it was finished by the time of his death five years later. At any rate, the house which stands today is in all essentials the house as he conceived it, and we should regard Parham as an exceptionally fine illustration of the ideas of comfort and elegance which appealed to a man of position in the middle years of Queen Elizabeth I.

He knew instinctively that it must be symmetrical, the mark of a house built virtually from scratch and of a man who knew his own mind. Its symmetry is not mechanical. There are no string-courses or parapets to emphasize floor or roof levels, and the gables and dormers zig-zagging along the main front are paired off in a regular pattern but with variations of size and pitch which preclude monotony. The chimneys are placed haphazard as need demanded. There is much play with bays and re-entrants. The porch, later several times rebuilt but occupying the same position, is by its modesty an indication of Sir Thomas Palmer's own character. The whole house suggests companionableness. It sets out to satisfy, not to startle. The effect aimed at and achieved is one of welcome and stability. It sits fair on its plot, rising from the grass without either plinth or steps, but postulating durable foundations and a very solid core.

Ladderlike the mullioned windows climb the façades. Some of them occupy almost the whole width and depth of bays, others belong in dormers, while the tallest light the great hall to the left of the entrance. There is not a curved line, not a single exterior ornament, of Elizabethan date. The patterns are made up of squares, oblongs and triangles. Parham is not in the least fanciful. It emerges from its immediate Gothic past to proclaim that the structure of a large house does not demand towers, buttresses and heavy blind walls. Windows need not be mere cavities to admit light and air, but can demonstrate by their very size and fragility the inner strength of good building and form its most natural and variable decoration. The whole external design is conceived around them, and although today only the windows of the hall are the originals, the others are close enough to them in spirit to teach us the lessons of good fenestration which Sir Thomas and his contemporaries taught themselves.

Windows mean rooms. One can match the style and general arrangement of the rooms at Parham in a dozen other Elizabethan houses, but nowhere else will you find them flowing so easily one into the next, maintaining the same scale throughout, although one will be high and airy and its neighbour intimate, and all of them drawing into the house light and freshness from the park outside. There were certain rooms which a house of that date and size was bound to contain – a great hall, a long gallery, a parlour, a solar and innumerable rooms for servants and storage – all of them except the gallery deriving from mediaeval tradition. Sir Thomas Palmer combined them in a way which is much nearer our own conception of a house than he would have known in his youth, or indeed than the vast Jacobean houses which were built twenty or thirty years later. Parham is structurally little

changed, but remains supremely habitable. You can eat in its hall, walk in its gallery, sleep in its bedrooms, even cook in its kitchen, without any sense that one century is being strained to fit the mould of another.

The best example of it is the Great Hall. It makes upon every visitor an immediate impression of fitness. Here is no baronial refectory open to the rafters, heavy with timber and gargoyles, cold, forbidding and feudal. It is a clean room – clean not merely in the sense of dusted and unlittered, but clean in its lines and proportions, cleansed by light from the southern windows, clean in its crisp combination of stone, wood and glass. It is unfussy, bold and certain. Perhaps we are seeing it today in a finer state than it ever was before, since the clutter has been removed, the oak stripped of paint, and the walls hung with a more splendid set of Tudor portraits than Sir Thomas is likely to have possessed. But its basic merit, like its structure, is his. It is very English. Although we know from *graffiti* scored in the plaster of an upper chamber that Dutch craftsmen were employed at Parham in the 16th century, the house is too early to have been affected by the tortuous foreign strapwork and outraged torsoes which over-burdened English wood and plasterwork soon afterwards. Instead we have an oak screen incorporating Corinthian pilasters and pierced by two finely sprung archways ; beautifully scaled pendants hanging from an ornamental ceiling ; panelling along half the height of the walls ; and the royal coat-of-arms dated 1593. There is no minstrels' gallery, no dais, and a comparatively modest fireplace. But to remind one of the origin of such halls, there are three internal windows, one for the ladies of the house and two for the steward, from which they could look down upon the hall from upper rooms at either end.

ABOVE *The portrait of Edward VI is by Guillim Stretes, and hangs over the fireplace in the hall. The stonework of the fireplace is the original.* OPPOSITE *The hall is approximately a double cube in its proportions, which partly accounts for its feeling of serenity. Above the screen is one of the two windows from which the steward, in his room over the buttery, could keep an eye on the servants below. The long bench with fire-buckets beneath it is contemporary with the building.*

The other architectural glory of Parham is its Long Gallery. It is of exceptional size, 158 feet by 17 feet, contained in the roof and running the whole length of the house, so that its main windows are the windows of the great gables of the east and west fronts respectively. Other windows were contrived at intervals down each side, forming bays internally, dormers externally. As it was constructed at roof-level, its interior walls are built up by panels which stand away from the sloping roof-line leaving long triangular cavities behind, and the ceiling, which was originally either rounded or ribbed to conceal the converging slopes, has recently been remodelled in five contiguous planes, like the panels of an opened umbrella. Its floor is of broad planks laid crossways and left bare between occasional rugs. It is impossible to furnish such a room conventionally, since in our modern sense it is not a room at all ; it is more like the enclosed deck of a galleon. You did not sit in it. You walked in it. You still do. The chairs and tables are placed at intervals along the walls, down the middle, or in the bays, but nobody wants to rest at them for more than a minute or two before rising to walk to another part, or to look more closely at the pictures, the needlework or the view. The gallery is a *tour de force*, a splendid feat of carpentry, a combination of simplicity with ingenuity,—a gazebo, a pergola carried indoors and raised up sixty feet. The first view of it makes everyone gasp with sur-

ABOVE *The Long Gallery, which runs the full length of the house on the top storey. This picture shows barely half of its length. The problem of furnishing so awkward a room has been cleverly overcome by making use of period pieces of differing bulk and height. The panels, which are original, help to conceal the fact that the gallery is constructed in the roof, and the frequent bays, leading right and left to dormer windows, break up its great length.* OPPOSITE *The screen of the hall is a fine example of mid-Elizabethan design influenced by the Italian Renaissance, including Corinthian pilasters and the fanlike motif above the vase of Philadelphus.*

TOP *The Great Chamber, reconstructed by Clive Pearson in its original position with furniture of the period. The bed came from Wroxton Abbey in Oxfordshire. By tradition, the coverlet and bed-head were worked by Mary Queen of Scots.* ABOVE *A surprising room suddenly to come upon in this very Elizabethan house, but one of the loveliest. It was redecorated in the Adam manner by the Bysshop family in the late 18th century as a library and sitting-room, and was the only Georgian room to escape Victorian redecoration.*

prise that a house so sensible can contain something so extravagant. But this feeling is soon followed by a sense of wonder at its sureness and boldness. It is an ark. Its conception is as simple as its structure is sound.

Life at Parham in its earliest days did not stray between hall and gallery and up the broad staircase which connects them. It flowed round the smaller rooms, of which there were at least ten in the family's part alone, and another dozen beyond the servants' screen. The hall was indeed the centre of the house, physically and emotionally. But on the west of the ground floor Sir Thomas constructed withdrawing-rooms, including a Great Parlour, and above them bedrooms connected (but this is guesswork from the present groundplan) by corridors. The need for privacy was a determinant motive in his design, and just as the lower rooms vary in size and position according to function, so too do the bedrooms, which today with little modification still serve the needs and deserts of family and visitor, old and young. Parham is, and always was, a home as well as a house, as different in spirit from a mediaeval manor as a well-constructed novel from a Book of Hours.

The creators of this work of art did not live in it for long. The baby into whose hands was thrust that ceremonial trowel in 1577 grew up to become a sea-dog serving Drake and Hawkins, and sold Parham in 1601 to Thomas Bysshop, a London merchant, whose descendants continued to inhabit the house for the next three hundred years. The fortunes of the Bysshops (who later reclaimed the defunct barony of Zouche), and the changes which they made to the house, need not greatly concern us, for only here and there – in the charming Adam saloon, in the stable-courts, and in the less happy rearrangement of the north front – can one still see their handiwork. Much of their interior reconstruction and decoration has been swept away during the last forty-five years, for in 1922 Parham found a rescuer whose name deserves to be bracketed with that of Sir Thomas Palmer himself.

He was Clive Pearson, younger son of the first Viscount
Cowdray. He bought Parham from the 17th Baroness Zouche,
and until his death in 1965, there was seldom a year when the
house was completely free of workmen, inside or out, and the
work still goes on today. He not only put it in order and provided
it with the conveniences (even electricity) which it hitherto
lacked, but restored to it with taste and infinite care that serenity
with which it was first endowed. He added greatly to its collection of works of art, above all portraits of the 16th- and 17th-
century English schools, which seem to give the house a second
set of occupants, an additional perspective into the past. The
rooms which he created by replacing a flight of windows here,
opening a doorway there, relaying floors which the Victorians
had torn out, or simply by removing paint and lumber and ornamental glass, are rooms which are as perfect expressions of our
contemporary taste as were Sir Thomas Palmer's of his.

*The south library, which is now the family's main
sitting-room. It was originally divided into two parts,
forming a buttery and a parlour. Clive Pearson remodelled the windows and opened up the original archway in the background leading to the dining-room.
The result is the most delightful room in the house.*

BELOW *The château is first seen at the end of a long avenue, formed partly by its great trees and outer courtyards, and partly by the village street, which ends approximately at the foot of the photograph.* LEFT *The back of the house is almost identical with the front, with the addition of tall shutters to the windows. Originally a bridge led centrally from the Salon to elaborate parterres, but both have now been abolished, and the rear of the house rises direct from the meadow-grass of radiating avenues.* RIGHT *Looking back from the highest point of the house, the belfry, one obtains an idea of how much ground is foreshortened in the photograph below. The village is at least half a mile away from the steps of the house, yet the broad avenue which it forms is an essential part of the design.*

Château de Balleroy

Normandy France 1626-36

The first surprise of Balleroy is that a complete village forms its avenue. Most great French houses were rebuilt on ancient sites, allowing little freedom for the realignment of the immediate surroundings, or are part of the villages which they dominate. But at Balleroy there was no house and no village until 1626, when François Mansart was commissioned by Jean de Choisy to build both in the middle of this radiant Norman farm and forestland. He made good use of the opportunity, siting the château on rising land and the village facing it across a shallow valley, and set the first two houses of the village on either side of the avenue as guides to what should be built later. His plan was followed, and with the aid of local byelaws it has been preserved unblemished to this day. The two rows of houses, set parallel and far apart, form by their perspective a frame to the château. Even after the Revolution, when certain of the villagers protested that the seigneur of Balleroy had no right to control the building-line of their cottages in order to improve his view, the avenue was saved by the argument that the cottagers also benefited by their view of the château. Thus aesthetics triumphed over politics to everybody's satisfaction, including our own, for the first sight of Balleroy from the north is one which delights every sense of fitness and design.

The road dips rather sharply as it passes through the village, and a cutting, or *dromos,* has been excavated to ease its gradient, leaving the broad cobbled shoulders of the avenue to ride over the natural curve of the ground on either side of the road. At its foot there is a wide open place where the public road bifurcates and the slow ascent to the château begins. The spacing of these various elements is very nicely calculated. The avenue formed by the village is very wide ; the gap between the village and the château is at least half a mile ; the contours of the ground are bold

and deep. Yet nobody could doubt, coming upon this view un-expectedly, that he had arrived at a group of buildings which had been conceived in relation to each other from the very start, and that the appearance of the house at the end of the avenue is enor-mously improved by its approach. Of course it is aristocratic. The village bears allegiance to the house. Even the ground plays its part in this tribute by dipping in a curtsy between house and village. But there is nothing servile about it. Village and château rise to the same level, on their separate hills, and each is a compliment to the other.

There is little in the village except its alignment to excite admiration. But the appearance of the château even from a mile away is intensely dramatic. It is a tall house in three sections, rising to a cupola on the roof, and its height is the most striking first impression that it makes. Clearly this must be the work of an architect of great daring, for although it retains the classical formula of a central block with two wings, the vertical dimen-sions are dangerously exaggerated in relation to the horizontal. Seeing it drawn out on paper, even Mansart must have had moments of hesitation. Those three separate roofs – should they not be joined into one to provide a stronger horizontal line ? That cupola – is it top-heavy ? Should there be lower pavilions at-tached to the house on each side to make the pyramidal intention a little more obvious ? If these thoughts ever entered his head, Mansart rejected them. The trees have grown up around the house to shelter its long limbs, but its verticality is still dominant and unashamed. Strong it is, but not elephantine. Very French, but classical. Grand, but not forbidding.

As you approach closer, three other elements of the design be-come more obvious. First, its colour. The bulk of the house is built of a ruddy schist stone, split into blocks of about the same size as bricks, for which at first glance they could be mistaken, and overlying these coppery courses are the regular long and short quoins of grey Caen masonry. Mansart made his effects by vol-umes and proportions and disdained the prettiness of surface smoothness and decoration. There is not a piece of carving, not even a wooden shutter, in the whole of this façade. Secondly, one

TOP *The designs of the young François Mansart were executed exactly, and nothing in this façade has been altered since it was built in 1626. The cross-section shows how large a part of the central block is occupied by the staircase which rises from directly inside the front door.* ABOVE *Part of the aesthetic appeal of Balleroy is due to the use of two contrasting types of stone. The main core is built of a coppery schist, but the windows and corners are emphasized by alternating long and short blocks of grey Caen stone, set in different planes.* OPPOSITE *The entrance front from the French garden on its approaches.*

ABOVE *The semi-circular steps connecting the two upper courtyards are examples of the care and originality of Mansart's work at Balleroy, and of the use he made of the different levels of the site.* OPPOSITE *Part of the 'defences' of the house, a relic of mediaevalism, but subtly transformed. The moat was never water-filled ; the circular sentry-boxes are little more than elegant punctuation-marks ; and the 'guard-room' on the right has become a garden pavilion.*

begins to notice the variations in strict formality which give the house its character. The opening of the front door is lower than the windows on each side of it, while the window on the first floor above the door is taller than any other. The roofs curve slightly, like a pagoda's, as they slope towards the eaves. The symmetry of the design is nowhere broken, and the impressiveness of the whole is due to its triadic structure – the pattern of a central feature flanked by lower supporters is frequently repeated, for instance in the arrangement of the dormer-windows – but it could no more be called a formal house than it could be called a pretty house. It is masculine and original. It is an astonishing work of art for an architect so young. Mansart was only 28 when he designed it, and apart from the Château de Berny, it was his first essay in domestic architecture.

The third element in the composition are the outlying buildings. The outriders begin with the village itself, but so dominant is the house that it is scarcely noticeable from a distance that on its immediate approaches there are other buildings set further back. They do not interrupt the view but add greatly to the visitor's sense of anticipation and grandeur as he advances to the front door. The approach is upwards, first by the central drive and finally by steps, and a series of bulwarks must be penetrated before entry into the house is granted. There is something military about this approach. It has the air of a fortress. Two round dungeon-towers (the right-hand tower is a columbarium, and the left-hand one an estate-lodging) flank the entrance wall and gate, the latter surmounted by a frieze of gilded spikes, gleaming like spears. This leads to a forecourt large enough to exercise a troop of cavalry, but now filled by *parterres* patterned from designs by Le Nôtre found at Vaux-le-Vicomte. A long stable block lies on each side ; they could be barracks. Next we cross the moat. This is no mere dip in the ground in deference to antiquity, but a full-throated chasm surrounding the house on all four sides, and although never water-filled, it is a most formidable and extensive obstacle. By now we have reached a second court, and see to right and left two domed sentry-boxes, and above them, linked by a balustrade, the most delightful features of Balleroy, two pavilions, in the same style as the house and highly domesticated, yet reminding one of the origins of such buildings in the outer turrets of mediaeval fortresses. Indeed, the whole complex is a subtle caricature of fortification. The moat was by then an extravagant anachronism, but it was a symbol of authority and added a new dimension (downwards) at an important point. The pepper-pot turrets have been lifted off the roof-level and re-used as garden ornaments. The guard-rooms have become summer-houses. And so on. This is mediaevalism's last flourish before the Gothic Revival. Its elements have been re-used to create a classical composition. It is brilliantly done.

Inside the château it is pure 17th century, but there is not quite the same certainty of touch as there is about the outside. The staircase, for instance, rises in straight flights round an open stair-well (the first in France to do so) immediately inside the front door, so that the stair is squashed rather awkwardly against

the windows. The banisters are of uncompromisingly heavy stone. The rooms do not always correspond to the fenestration : floor-levels will sometimes slice across windows in order to provide rooms low enough for family living. But the main rooms are splendid in a rather heavy way, particularly the Salon on the ground floor, which retains its panelling and carved *putti* and rosettes, all over-painted in a pleasing grey, and hung with some excellent mid 19th-century hunting-scenes by a former owner of the house, Comte Albert de Balleroy ; and above it, the Salon d'Honneur, which occupies the central bay on the park side of the house, a strong, well-proportioned room, richly coffered and decorated, with floral swags against the wall both painted and carved, and hung with royal portraits by Pierre Mignard – an astonishing collection of proud men, women and children, with the bloom of purple grapes about their clothes and persons, and adopting attitudes and expressions which make them almost as intolerable in paint as they must have been in the flesh. There are other rooms less formidable, especially the dining room with its 18th-century *boiserie,* and a little sitting room which proves that a strongly carved ceiling and cornice can still make satisfactory decorations even in a confined space.

The Château de Balleroy is the best preserved and least altered of any of François Mansart's country houses. Externally there has been no change at all. The replacement of French *parterres* behind the house by an 'English' parkscape in the 19th century was an improvement, since it fits in well with the lovely beech avenues which were planted on Mansart's instructions in a chequerboard pattern over quite a large part of the surrounding countryside. The château itself survived 18th- and 19th-century replanning. It survived (because the then *châtelaine* feigned a mortal and highly infectious illness) the French Revolution. Even more remarkably it survived the Allied invasion of Normandy in June 1944, when the Americans, advancing south from Omaha Beach, only fifteen miles away, spared the château because it was in use as a German hospital. To these happy chances, and to the concern and taste of the present owners, Monsieur and Madame Hubert Bénédic, we owe our enjoyment of one of the most beautiful buildings in the whole of France.

Château d'Oiron

Deux-Sèvres France c.1515-1640

The site of this magnificent 17th-century house is so unemphatic that you come upon it quite unawares in the wide plain of Poitou. There is no preparation for the surprise of its sudden emergence from the fields and the simple village which shares its name. There it stands, battered but serene, apparently detached from its surroundings, giving the village nothing, drawing from it nothing, with no park and almost no garden, and proudly indifferent to the modest houses beyond the wall. Only the church, built at the same time and by the same family, shares something of the patrician exclusiveness of the château. Both were defaced in the Revolution, and it is not wholly surprising. Oiron is a proud, disdainful house. It has the elegance, but also some of the coldness, of the aristocracy which created it.

It has not been inhabited for some twenty years, and the interior is empty of furniture and falling apart at the seams. But it is far from ruinous, and what damage has been caused by time is being slowly made good by the Beaux Arts. It illustrates admirably the problem of great houses which no longer belong to families with sufficient interest or wealth to maintain them. Has a house, like a tree, a natural term of life, beyond which it is absurd to prop it up? Or is a house of this quality a work of art which must be preserved indefinitely at almost any cost? Most nations of the West have accepted the latter view, if only because houses like Oiron will never be built again. As the art-form itself

RIGHT *A central gateway leads from the public road to the strong architecture of the façade, which is softened by two cedars standing on either side of the approachway.* TOP *A portrait of Artus Gouffier, the builder of the Rennaissance part of Oiron, in the church. He was a favourite of François I and died in 1519.*

has vanished, any surviving specimens of it must be unique. But devotion to the past can be carried too far. If nobody can find a use for a house like Oiron, the vast expense of maintaining it whole could not be justified by any government. So there must be selective maintenance – of the fabric, of the main elevations, of some chosen rooms. This, in fact, is what is occurring. It would cost some ten million francs to restore Oiron to its full glory. But by selective repair enough can be saved to suggest what that glory once was.

The house is built in the form of a square open on one side and surrounded on all four by a wide moat. A 14th-century castle once stood here, and one of its towers can still be seen enfolded by the later tower which replaced it. The decision to rebuild the place was made in about 1515 by Artus Gouffier, the favourite of François I, and continued after his death in 1519 by his widow and his son, Claude Gouffier, who also rose high in the service of his king. Claude's grandson, Louis Gouffier, rebuilt part of the house in the taste of 1630-40. In the 19th century heavy restoration was carried out to the exterior but without altering its character. What we see, therefore, is a combination of early French Renaissance with the mid-17th century, both of them executed in the grandest style of the day, and, what is most important, in the same stone, the *tuffeau* of the Loire valley, which is faintly buttery outside but whitens with age inside. The consistent use of this lovely stone gives the whole house an architectural unity which it could not otherwise have possessed.

As you approach the house between two little lodges, you see the main block ahead of you, a great cliff of stone heavily decorated and rusticated, with tall windows through which daylight can be seen on the far side – obviously a great room lies here on the first floor – and above it is an attic storey three windows wide standing palely against the huge blue tent of the roof. On each side of the central block is a square pavilion of three storeys, that on the left surmounted by a huge block of stone carved with panoplies, as if the arms of the dozen noblest families in France had been compressed into a single package by an arms-crushing machine. All this is the work of the mid-17th century; the main block and the right-hand pavilion date from about 1640, and the left-hand pavilion from some thirty years later.

Down each side of the *cour d'honneur* is a wing at right-angles to the central block terminating in a great round tower. That to the right is no more than a ruinous orangery, and the tower a shell, for the upper floors were removed after 1667 to form a terrace. This is one of the few important features which Oiron has lost from the original building, and the result is unfortunate, for it gives the courtyard on this side a mean, unfinished look, and the tower is out of scale with the building that links it to the main building. However, it matters little, since every eye is drawn to the other side of the courtyard, to the long Renaissance wing which is Oiron's chief glory, inside and out.

The round tower at the near end of it is not part of Artus Gouffier's design, having been added by his great-grandson, Louis, more than a century later. What we owe to Artus is the

ABOVE *The extent of Oiron seen from the forecourt. The whole central block belongs to the 17th century, but was built in two periods, the main house in about 1640, and the left-hand pavilion, surmounted by stone panoplies, after 1667. The loveliest feature of Oiron, however, is the Renaissance wing on the left, here seen obliquely. The round tower was added in the 17th century to match the mediaeval tower on the other side, here concealed by the cedar.* OPPOSITE *The back of the house, with its earlier moat. It has not been inhabited for twenty years, but the Beaux Arts is gradually restoring the fabric.* BELOW *The elaborate coat-of-arms in the pediment over the central block. They are the arms of Louis XIII.*

conception of an open arcade on the ground floor surmounted by two storeys of palatial proportions and divided externally into bays by columns extended upwards by tall niches for statues. Above the arches are circular recesses containing terracotta busts of Roman emperors, and eleven widely spaced windows, six of them with glass panes, five blank. As this fine wing was being built, Renaissance influences were flooding in and Claude Gouffier succeeded his father. It therefore starts off Gothic, in the vaulting of the arcade, and ends classical, in the surface-decoration and the siting of the main windows. The splendid *œil-de-bœuf* windows in the roof are 17th-century additions. There can be few better examples in all France of the fusing of mediaeval with classical elements to produce an entirely satisfactory result. From one end the columns of the façade, with their twisted flutings, appear like the buttresses of a late mediaeval chapel; from in front they could be ornamental piers forming a classic colonnade. Along the lower cornice is several times repeated the tag from Virgil HIC TERMINUS HAERET, the words which Dido spoke to Aeneas on his arrival in Latium – 'Here will you remain' – and one finds it again and again in the surviving parts of the Renaissance interior. Thus did Louis Gouffier impress on himself and his descendants his satisfaction with the house that he and his father had made. It was a nobleman's retreat, a fit place for his last years, a worthy legacy to his successors.

Above the ground-floor arcade of this wing is a long gallery which extends its full length. This enormous room has windows down each side, and a fireplace at one end, but is otherwise a rectangular box without structural variation. It could be monotonous, but the ceiling is broken up by cross-beams and the walls by the window-shutters which open inwards in four sections, one above the other, like bats, and create pleasing effects by alternating bars of shadow and squares of light which may or may not have been deliberate. The main decoration of the room is painted. Thirteen huge frescoes of scenes from the siege of Troy occupy the

OPPOSITE *The long east wing of Oiron, begun by Artus Gouffier in about 1515, is carried on an open arcade of semi-Gothic style, with buttresses on the courtyard side faced by twisted pillars. Only this ground floor was finished by the time of his death, and the upper part of the wing was completed in a more classical style by his son, Claude.* BOTTOM *The Salle des Gardes, which takes up the whole of the first floor of the Renaissance wing. It is more than 150 feet in length. The 'barbaric fireplace' (*BELOW*) at the far end of the gallery dates from the early 16th century, and carries the motto,* Hic Terminus Haeret.

TOP *The magnificent stone stairway of the Renaissance part of Oiron, built in 1544, was preserved inside the 17th-century additions. The treads are each three yards wide and formed of a single block of stone.* ABOVE *Some of the 17th-century decoration, which is now flaking and cracking, still reminds the visitor of the stupendous scale and richness of the house.* OPPOSITE *The Cabinet des Muses, one of the more delicately decorated rooms in the house. Pairs of pillars, striped blue and white, separate figures of young girls playing musical instruments.*

panels facing the windows down each side, and the ceiling is divided up into painted squares, of which there are some six hundred in all. None of this painting is of very high quality. The frescoes are in the Italian mannerist style of the 1540-50 period and are probably by Noel Jallier. The ceiling squares are mid-17th century. The latter are crude little landscapes, or buildings, or flowers, or (when invention gave out) the initials of Louis Gouffier, or lame jokes, like a picture of three men sitting on asses with the caption *Nous sommes sept* – the reader being invited to include himself in this foolish company. But collectively the painting adds distinction to the room. It is not in the least gaunt or over-burdened. The barbaric fireplace only arouses relief that the whole room was not similarly decorated in three dimensions.

In the 17th-century rooms of the main block the decorators did not show equal forbearance. The grossest, most tasteless, form of heavy gilding is combined with carving on a scale far too big for the rooms. Swags of flowers and fruit hang lumpishly from the rafters, and the fireplaces stride out into the rooms like stage-settings. The ceiling panels are crude and mannerist, and the columns between the wall-panels are painted blue and gold in alternate flutings. Only in the *Cabinet des Muses* is there sufficient delicacy and restraint to persuade one that the owners who commissioned so elegant an exterior for the château were the same people who decorated it inside. It is certainly not improved by decay and the absence of all comfort. To sit on the floor – for there is not a single chair – in these rooms is to experience disillusion with the French 17th century. But then look through any window at any façade of the building, and confidence will be restored that in line and proportion and stone-carving the Château d'Oiron is the equal of any other in the famous valley of the Loire. It is almost unknown to the ordinary tourist. *Michelin* reserves for it his most uninviting symbol: 'interesting'. It is worth a great deal more than that, for of two centuries, the 16th and the 17th, it remains a monument of quite exceptional worth.

Villa Doria-Pamphilj *Rome Italy 1644-52*

The Villa turns its back to Rome and its pleasantest face towards the garden and the park. The magnificent view of the dome of St Peter's, barely a mile away, is seen only from the entrance drive and part of the roof. This exclusion of the city, this pretence of *rus in urbe,* is deliberate, for the house was built as a retreat, for quiet domesticity and selective entertainment, and was appropriately named a *casino,* which suggests exactly the right combination of frivolity with a cultivation of the arts and a growing love of nature, characteristic of the 17th century in Rome.

The site is on part of the Janiculum, west of the Tiber, and is reputedly the place chosen by the Emperor Galba for his own villa, which would account for the great richness of Roman sculpture disinterred from its grounds. Not only is it poised high above Rome, favoured by sea breezes which gave it the name of *Belrespiro,* but its large park, six miles round and an astonishing private lung so near the centre of a great city, is full of steep valleys and natural knolls. The park is large enough for an afternoon's drive without once venturing outside its walls, and paintings show that elaborate hunts once took place through its glades. It is still the biggest of the Roman villa-parks, and one of the best pre-served. Today there are no huntsmen, very few people and almost no traffic within it. It looks curiously like an English park, with ornamental plantings and an occasional architectural feature like a fountain or a belvedere, and some lodges and little farmhouses scattered between the trees. Herds of sheep and goats move slowly through the glades, attended by rustic figures who might have been lifted from romantic landscape paintings of three hundred years ago, adopting Theocritean attitudes as they pause, sunk in apparent contemplation, by a waterfall. It is exceedingly beautiful.

OPPOSITE *The villa was designed in about 1644 for Camillo Pamphilj, probably by Algardi. The garden originally extended to the lower level, but this is now left rough and grazed by sheep. The park surrounds the house on all but the entrance side, from where* (ABOVE) *the dome of St Peter's can be seen beyond the gate-piers. The entrance to the house* (TOP) *is monumental, both architecturally and in the number of Roman statues and bas-reliefs employed on the façade.* OVERLEAF *The villa was built for pleasure and entertaining, and for housing part of the fabulous Doria art collection. But it is best known today for the garden. There are three terraces: the upper at the entrance level; the middle terrace containing the main parterre; and the lowest at the foot of the steps shown in the foreground.*

TOP *The mass of sculpture on the garden façade of the Villa Doria is in imitation of the Palazzo Borghese.* ABOVE '*A grotto, half-classical with columns, half-romantic with shells and pebbling, and a statue of a goddess in its shadowed apse over whose face passes the rippled light reflected from the water in which she stands.*' OPPOSITE *A staircase connecting the upper with the middle level of the garden. Here too sculpture in the round and as bas-reliefs was used extensively, much of it coming from the surrounding hills, where the Emperor Galba is reputed to have had his villa.*

The villa itself, however, could not belong to any other country but Italy, and yet for Italy it is an unusual building. Its design is simple, a heightened cube of moderate size surmounted by a rectangular belvedere. This simplicity is deceptive, for in several ways its dimensions are more elaborate than they first appear. For one thing, it is taller on the garden side than at the entrance, taking advantage of the fall of the ground to gain an extra storey. For another, a bay has been added the full height of the main block on this same side, and an entrance archway of unusual height encloses the front door. The belvedere, too, by being recessed from the façades at roof-level, gives the house extra movement, but so delicate are the proportions of the remainder, that the belvedere might be considered architecturally unnecessary, even a blemish, for it is blunt and rather plain. If you eliminate it in imagination by placing a thumb over it in the photograph, the toylike quality of the house is enhanced. It is a pavilion, though of considerable size, and depends for its effect on its situation, its clean lines and the subtle use of antique sculpture.

On no other house in Italy have carved tablets and statues in the round been applied so generously to the exterior. Each façade is a vertical art-gallery. If this ornament were to be described in words only, the reader would be aghast at the overload of sculpture which he would picture in his mind. In fact, it fuses beautifully with its background. The tablets become friezes, the free figures take the place of the far heavier columns and pediments which one would find on other Roman houses of this date. There is no sense of encrustation, nor of over-sentimentality. It remains a late Renaissance house, not a glorification of old Rome. Statues of Roman senators in niches beside the doors, busts set in circular depressions around the façades, are decorative, not formal, because the niches are shadowed, and the sculpture does not obtrude. They can be noticed, or unnoticed, like flunkeys posted up a grand staircase, but their presence adds a note of richness which is muted by the scale of the whole arrangement. It is a novel, and utterly satisfying, device.

The house drops into its garden. There are three levels – the upper entrance level, the level of the *giardino segreto* or *parterre*, and the 'theatre garden' at the bottom, which is now left fairly rough. Each is divided from the one above by a retaining wall and connected by staircases with ornamented balustrades. It was, and remains, the grandest garden of its day. The centre of it is the middle level, now patterned by low box hedges arranged in whorls and scrolls, seen best from the house or from one of the encircling terraces on the upper level, since the *parterre* is confusing when viewed from its own centre, and the whole composition of house and garden needs to be taken in at a glance. Of course it is formal, and was probably even more formal when first laid out in the rigid geometrical lines of 17th-century patterning. It is not a garden for flowers or many surprises, but it is a garden for movement, vertically and horizontally, up and down the different levels or along their gravel paths, and at each point there is a further parade of sculpture or huge terracotta orange-pots, some of them set on the wide steps or along the parapets of the balus-

trades. There is also a moderate use of water. Towards one end of the *parterre* you find an ornamental pool; below its centre, and incorporated in the lower retaining wall, a grotto, half-classical with columns, half-romantic with shells and pebbling, and a statue of a goddess in its shadowed apse over whose face passes the rippled light reflected from the water in which she stands.

Then outwards from the formal garden, in ever-increasing degrees of rustification, extend exedras and fountains, isolated stone vases, griffon-ended seats within circular box-hedges, gates and little statues, either Roman originals or Italian copies of them, so that it is often difficult to tell what is two thousand years old, and what three hundred, so sympathetically are the different styles blended with each other. So we reach the park, which defiantly keeps at bay the encircling houses of new Rome, and pass an ornamental pool and dripping cascades, which were the contributions of the late 18th century to this romantic fancy. There suddenly in the grass is a fountain of twisted dolphins by Bernini; here a grotto tunnelled beneath flowing water; here a pair of elaborate classical gates leading nowhere except to the further stretches of the park; and everywhere the woods, judiciously thinned to reveal the views, and occasionally at the end of a vista a pink fragment of the Villa.

The Villa was built in the middle of the 17th century by Algardi, probably assisted by Gian Francesco Grimaldi, for Camillo Pamphilj, nephew of Pope Innocent X. Camillo, following the practice of those days, was appointed a Cardinal, but protested to his uncle that 'much as I admire the virtue of chastity, I feel unable to practise it without a wife', and gave up his Cardinal's hat to marry in 1647 the gay and vivacious Olimpia, Princess of Rossano. They spent their honeymoon in the casino at Caprarola. The Villa Pamphilj on the family's estate on the Janiculum was probably begun in 1644, the year when Giambattista Pamphilj became Pope Innocent X, and both house and garden were finished by 1652. It has been little changed since then. Recently the house has been sold by the Dorias to the State, but is let to the Belgian Ambassador as his residence.

It is one of the most delightful houses in Rome. Internally it contains no rooms of great magnificence, and apart from some good original stuccos on walls and ceilings, its decoration has suffered from restoration. But externally it is a little jewel, which could be taken as the ideal of the Italian villa from which so many other nations have borrowed. It owes its deserved fame to the family which built it, the archaeological treasures which it incorporates, and the relationship of house to garden – a tray held at waist-level and filled with flowers.

ABOVE *Part of the park of the Villa Doria, where one continually comes across fountains or waterfalls created during one period or another of the long occupation of the villa by men of wealth and culture. This is one of the late 18th-century additions.* OPPOSITE *'It looks curiously like an English park, with ornamental plantings and an occasional architectural feature like a fountain or a belvedere ... Herds of sheep and goats move slowly through the glades.' Part of the villa itself is seen at the end of this vista.*

Skokloster *near Uppsala Sweden 1650-68*

ABOVE *A wooden model of the house, contemporary with its building. Since then, no alterations have been made to the exterior apart from the removal of the dormers, and few within. The house is completely square, with a square central courtyard, and the only difference between the four façades are the steps and pediment on the entrance front, seen on the right of the model.* OPPOSITE *The house stands on a narrow arm of Lake Mälar, which stretches northwards towards Uppsala. Here it is seen from the opposite shore. In the trees to the right of the main building is the little white mediaeval house in which Herman Wrangel, father of the builder of Skokloster, lived until his death in 1643.*

It is a big-boned house. This is not merely to say that it is cliff-like and many-roomed, but that its proportions are as sturdy within as without. You will not find much delicacy here, even in the detail, but what you will find is an extraordinary boldness of treatment, a galleon style of building, which in the mass is deeply impressive. When you add to this the fact that the decoration and contents were outstanding in their own day and have not since been disturbed, you have a rarity. Skokloster may seem rather a forbidding house from the outside or from the base of its central courtyard. The first few rooms, too, may shock by their self-assertiveness. But to see the whole house for the second or third time is to experience a translation to the mid-17th century, to comprehend the bridge between the Gothic and the Classic, and to know just what it felt like to tread bare boards or to lift the heavy curtains of a four-poster bed three hundred years ago.

If one seeks an additional argument for preserving the great houses of Europe, one will find it here in the picture which it gives of a vanished age. It can be given in no other way. A fortune has been spent, and rightly spent, in raising from the bed of Stockholm's harbour the warship *Vasa* which sank there in 1628. It is a wonderful historic document. But it is nothing in comparison to Skokloster, which was built soon after the *Vasa* for one of Sweden's greatest men, Count Carl Gustav Wrangel, and has suffered no damage and scarcely any alteration since then. The only regret which a foreign visitor must express is that when financial necessity forced its sale to the Government in 1967, the descendants of Wrangel, the family of von Essen, were not allowed to remain in the house as its curators. Skokloster is now a lifeless, if not a soulless, museum.

It lies on one of the many arms of Lake Mälar between Stockholm and Uppsala, actually on a peninsula, but it might be an island, so conscious is one of the enveloping presence of water and its importance for communications in summer and (as an ice-road) in winter. It is a four-storeyed square house with octagonal towers at each corner and a square courtyard acting as a light-well in the middle. Eleven windows stretch between the towers

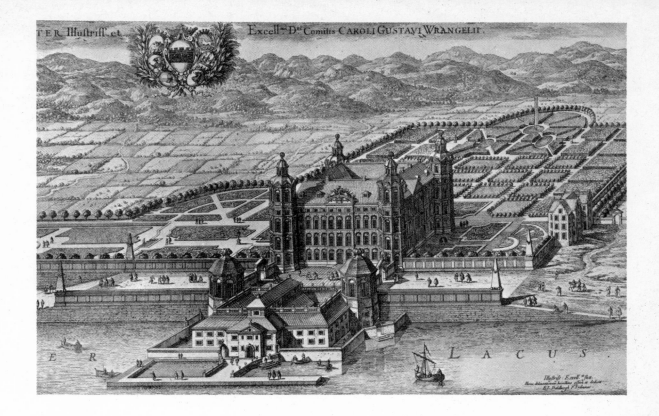

and five along each inner side of the court: once an elevation had been drawn it was repeated exactly for the others. There is no variation even for the front door, which is merely a window elongated, and the only way in which the entrance façade was distinguished from the others was by the Wrangel arms and panoply high above. Yet this uncompromising building is not without elegance. The blind arches above all the main windows add the interest which eyebrows add to the human face, while the canopies of the towers have the pageantry of standards flowing from a pavilion's roof. Count Wrangel was a soldier and Admiral, and only subsequently a statesman, and one can find reflected in the design of this building something of the austerity of his campaigns. His architect was a Frenchman, Jean de la Vallée, with details by Nicodemus Tessin, a north-German. But we can be quite certain that Wrangel impressed his own personality on the building. The equestrian portrait of him by David Klöker (Ehrenstrahl) which hangs in the drawing-room is sufficient indication that he was a man who knew, and got, what he wanted. It was built during the prime of his life, between 1650 and 1668, but when he died in 1676, some of the interior was still unfinished, including the great hall. It remains bare to its rafters to this very day, none of his descendants having had the money or the temerity to complete the great man's work.

The only part of the house which is out of character with the remainder is found immediately inside the front door. Here four pairs of double Ionic columns support the vaulted roof of the entrance portico. It is not surprising to learn that they came from Italy, though given their final polish in Stockholm, for they are of excellent workmanship and design, and they impart a classical elegance to the courtyard which is otherwise monastic and rather plain. The idea of a central arcaded court was, of course, a

TOP *An engraving by Eric Dahlbergh, made in about 1670, which indicates how Count Wrangel intended to complete Skokloster and its garden. The very elaborate harbour buildings in the foreground, including a covered staircase to the terrace level, were never erected. On the right is Herman Wrangel's little manor.* ABOVE *An equestrian portrait of Fieldmarshal Count Carl Gustav Wrangel (1613-76), painted in 1662 by David Klöker, who later took the name of Ehrenstrahl when he was knighted.* OPPOSITE *The magnificent stucco ceiling of the King's Room (the Count's ceremonial dining-hall) was made by John Zauch in 1664. The centre-piece shows Daniel's struggle with the Babylonian dragon, who holds in his mouth the hook for the chandelier.*

favourite one in the Italian Renaissance. But unless the court is very large or the surrounding buildings low, the effect is apt to be prison-like. At Skokloster its starkness is emphasised by closing in the upper corridors which frame it (in the warmer climate of Italy they would probably have been left open), and by the roughness of the cobbling and rain-conduits which form the central square. Already we are prepared for the juxtaposition of strong and boldly shaped materials which mark the character of the interior.

The stair-steps are single lengths of red limestone, mounting easily to each of the three upper floors with star-vaulting above and balusters, partly in the round, partly in *trompe l'œil*, on each side of the ascent. The landings are a great feature of the house, for they ring the entire circuit of the courtyard on each floor and provide places for walking as well as connecting corridors to the various rooms. They are decorated in the liveliest style. On the first floor tall portraits are placed between the windows, portraits of officers serving under the command of Herman Wrangel, the father of the more famous Carl Gustav, and hence antedating the house itself. On every convenient panel left in the corridor-walls the Count had admonitory inscriptions painted in a bold black cursive script. They appear in several languages, but a majority are in Latin. In places a motto can be detected underneath the later motto by which the Count replaced it after further reflexion or experience of the world. Even so, he did not always follow his own precepts. *Melius unum civem servare quam mille hostes occidere* ('Better to save one' fellow-citizen than to kill a thousand enemies') we read, in the house of the greatest warrior of 17th-century Sweden. And *Sine sanitate nulla felicitas* ('There is no happiness without health') seems a strange conclusion for a semi-palace which contained not a single bathroom or water-closet. But whatever their moral uplift, the decorative effect of these panels is very high. So are the portraits of the first nineteen Roman Emperors painted above the doors in grisaille, and the treatment of the planks forming the ceiling. All this paint is now rather faded : it has flaked in strips from around the Emperors, making them appear as if in rapid motion from right to left. But as the paintings were rather roughly executed, their slight deterioration is an improvement. These unintentional 'long galleries', so well lit, so plainly but amusingly decorated, such a convenience to a house built in this shape, would draw the visitor

TOP *The library on the top floor of Skokloster. The lattice doors of narrow wooden rails which close the bookcases probably date from the early half of the 18th century.* ABOVE *The courtyard in the centre of the house. Cobbled drainage-channels lead to a central grid-covered well. Arcades surround the courtyard, which, like the exterior of the house, is symmetrical on all sides.* OPPOSITE *One of the four galleries on the first floor. The windows on the left look onto the central courtyard. Between them Count Wrangel placed portraits of officers who had served his father in the 1620s, among them, nearest the camera, a Scotsman, Colonel David Drummond. Some of Count Wrangel's mottoes are seen below the windows and portraits.*

ABOVE *The most magnificent room at Skokloster, the King's Room, is so-called from the portraits of all the Swedish kings which hang against the embossed leather of the walls. The carved wooden fireplace (1663) was later supplemented by the stove on its right, faced with blue, green and white tiles.* BELOW *In the small dining-room, as elsewhere throughout the house, great importance is given to the ceiling and fireplace. The stuccoed laurel-leaves of the ceiling were made by Nils Erikson in 1672, and the sculpture of the fireplace by Marcus Hebel in 1657-8.* OPPOSITE *Skokloster contains a unique set of joiner's tools from the mid-17th century. It is said that they were the personal tools of Count Wrangel, and nobody was allowed to touch them, except the master himself.*

back to them again and again even if the arrangement of the rooms did not necessitate it.

All these rooms are of moderate but not modest size. As the great hall was never finished, the lack of any really big reception room is still felt. On the other hand, there appear never to have been any closets which today would make small sitting-rooms or bedrooms. The bedrooms were in fact large even for a four-poster, and because the majority of them had windows only on one side, they are rather dark. The four angle-towers provide bonus-rooms, for, when one thinks that the end-room of the house has been reached, there opens up the capacious octagon of the tower which is always well-lit by windows on seven of the eight sides. On the top floor the ceiling is lower than on the other three, and here the rooms are smaller. From a whole series of them the library was contrived, and at this level the house changes completely in character from roomy and self-assertive to intimate and secluded. The library is a compartmentalized gallery and houses a unique collection of books; it alone would justify Skokloster's reputation as the greatest private house in Sweden. Other rooms on this level contain the equally famous collection of arms and armour, collected partly by Count Wrangel, and partly by his successors, the Brahes and Bielkes.

Below, the main decorative features of the house are the ceilings and the fireplaces. These are both on a big scale. The stuccoists were mostly Italian, but the most splendid ceiling of all was executed in the King's Room (the Count's dining-room) by the German, Johan Zauch, in 1664, and there can be few examples of such flamboyant early-baroque to be seen elsewhere in Europe. Gaudily-painted animals and representations of the four continents are attached to the ceiling by one wing or limb. The central dragon holds the chandelier in its mouth, forever threatening to let go. The whole ceiling is a riot of sculpture and colour, at which generations of diners and tourists have gaped, twisting their necks sideways in attitudes as painful as the dragon's to get a better view. The fireplace in this room, as in others, is more sober. They are big features, boldly modelled in painted wood like major pieces of furniture. But functionally they were inadequate: a few years after the house was finished, auxiliary stoves of iron and faience were added alongside the fireplaces to raise the temperature of the rooms by a few extra degrees. This duplication is awkward, but typical of a period when households were run like battalions, and decoration was subordinate to convenience.

The riches of this house deserve, and have received, catalogues divided into sections each worthy of a separate museum. Many of the contents were looted from the parts of northern Europe over-run by the Field Marshal's campaigns. Others were gifts from his admirers, and still more were added by the Brahe family, like the lovely tapestries presented by Louis XIV to the Swedish Ambassador in Paris. The collection, like the house, was entailed and never dispersed. But it is more surprising that the whole of the 18th and 19th centuries passed without the owners of Skokloster redecorating the rooms or rearranging them. They recognised, as we do, that here is an extraordinary survival from a golden age.

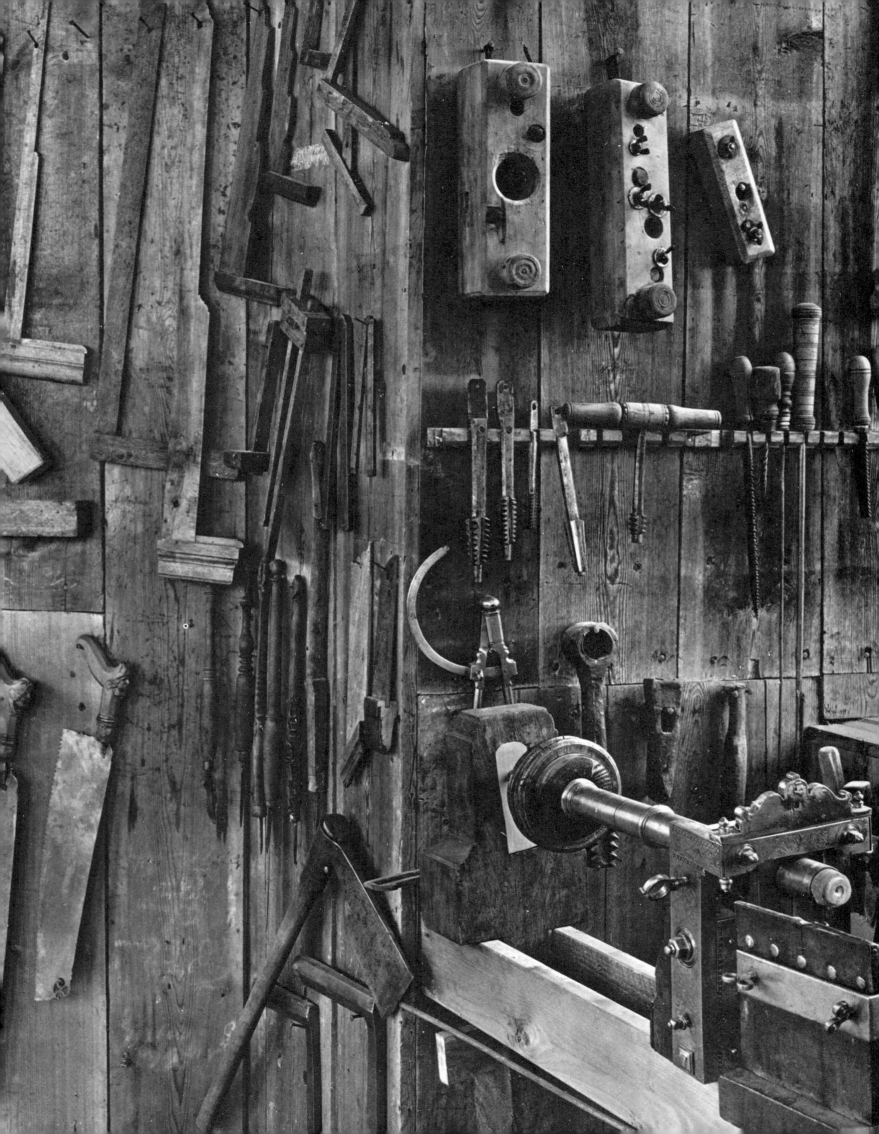

Vranov-nad-Dyji
Moravia Czechoslovakia c.1690

ABOVE *In the late 18th century a porcelain factory was founded in association with the castle. This vase carried a picture of Vranov seen from the north.*
OPPOSITE *Vranov stands on a rocky pinnacle above the River Dyji. The site was originally occupied by a mediaeval fortress, and one of its towers can be seen in the right-centre. In the 1680s, Fischer von Erlach, who became Court architect to the Emperor of Austria, constructed the huge oval Ancestors' Hall on the crown of the rock, in place of the old chapel for which he substituted the building on the far right of the group.*

The house is known equally well by its German name, Schloss Frain, for this is the part of Moravia which lies alongside the Austrian border, and historically its connections with Vienna have been as strong as those with Prague. The countryside is very beautiful. It is hilly more than mountainous, and the forests trail off into the meadows like garlands of flowers, leaving broad shoulders of land where the corn stands stiff and ruddy. The River Dyji (the Austrian Thaya) has dug a deep channel through the woods, and at one point, only a mile from the border, it has exposed a high cliff so precipitous that one of the towers of the castle drops straight to the river and water could be drawn up it as if from a well.

Other mediaeval towers ring the escarpment, and the oldest of them, dating from the 13th century, still stands guard at the entrance. But it is not as a fortress that Vranov is now celebrated. On the most prominent point of the rock, like the figurehead of a schooner, rises a building which it is amazing to find in so gothic a position. It is part of the later Schloss which was built at the end of the 17th century by the greatest of the Austrian baroque architects, Fischer von Erlach.

Fischer's patron was Michael John II of Althan, who won distinction at the Austrian Imperial Court. In 1665 the Renaissance house on the site had been largely destroyed by fire, and when Michael Althan recovered the property in 1680 (his family having been dispossessed of it some sixty years before), he found little more surviving than the corner of the courtyard and the ruins of the mediaeval fortifications. He decided to rebuild. Fischer von Erlach was a bold choice as his architect, for in the 1680s he was not yet 30, and this was his first important commission. His design for the house must have staggered his patron, for the whole of it was subordinated to one room, called, appropriately for so theatrical a piece, the *Ahnensaal* or 'Hall of Ancestors'. This is the building that dominates the valley. It occupies the site formerly held by the chapel, which Fischer rebuilt in the rear and on a lower ledge of the rock. The gods were replaced by the ancestors, and the modest little chapel of the Althans by a flamboyantly baroque hangar.

From below (and here one means from 500 feet below) it is already clear that it is an oval building, a shape which remained Fischer's favourite, almost his signature. From this distance, it seems highly improbable that it could contain but one room, for it is of great size and there are three superimposed rows of windows – rectangular, oval and dormer. Two triumphal arches extend on either side like midget arms. If Fischer could see his youthful masterpiece now, he would be dismayed. The arches are not his : they were constructed as supports for the main walls, together with the terraces (a valuable addition), in 1787. The roof is not his : it dates from the mid-18th century. Fischer's roof was flattened above the oval windows and surrounded by a balustrade. The present mansard roof was no doubt erected because a flat roof, however complimentary to the building, would not bear the heavy weight of snow in winter, and the dormer windows inserted in it are false, opening inwards to nothing more than a huge timber cage above the dome. It remains from outside a building which would arouse astonishment in any position, but particularly when poised on such a precipice, its walls dropping flush with the walls of the cliff. Audacity of style and engineering could scarcely have gone further. It was the work of a young man in a hurry to make a reputation, and it was commissioned by a patron anxious to rival in showmanship the emperor himself.

The interior of the hall owes nothing to its site, for it is impossible to see out of the lower windows, which were glazed by

BELOW *The whole range seen from the north in a drawing of about 1790. The roof of the Ancestors' Hall (left) had already been altered to its present appearance ; it was previously flat. Between it and Fischer's chapel (centre) is the main range of living-rooms, forming a three-sided court open to the view. Below is the small town of Vranov with its bridge over the river.* OPPOSITE *The entrance to Vranov still passes over the mediaeval bridge clearly seen in the drawing below, and under the largest of the old castle's surviving towers. On the left is Fischer von Erlach's chapel, built 1698-1700. The twin towers were not part of his design, but were added in 1726.*

coloured glass in 1799. It owes everything to its shape; one might almost say, to its geometry. The basic oval is converted by its dome into a half-egg, split lengthwise. The dome does not rest conventionally on a drum, in which the *œils-de-bœuf* would normally have been placed, but rises directly from the walls. This arrangement has two results. First, the painted ceiling is brought a great deal closer to the spectator, giving him not so much a sense of height as a sense of being enveloped by colour. Secondly, the *œils-de-bœuf*, being ovals pierced through the lower part of an oval dome, acquire greatly increased depth and interest. There is no shape quite like them except eye-sockets in a human skull. So fascinated was Fischer by this interpenetration of circular shapes that he added further ones: a gallery running right round the base of the dome, passing through the reveals of the *œils-de-bœuf* by arched openings; and also round holes driven through the floor of the gallery to the ceilings of the windows below, rendering the gallery unusable unless the holes are bridged by planks. Every part of this complicated piece of solid geometry was painted in fresco by Michael Rottmayer, the Austrian, who also painted some of the ceilings at the palace of Pommersfelden.

All this is above the level of the walls. But seldom can there have been a domed hall of this size where the walls compete so successfully for attention with the dome itself. This is one of the glories of the hall: every part of it is lit with equal intensity by the twenty windows – ten above, ten below – and the interest is maintained from floor-level (which includes a marble chess-board scaled for human chessmen) to the culmination of Rottmayer's Apotheosis of the House of Althan high above. It is an Ancestors' Hall. So it must contain ancestors. There they stand, ten Althans in niches between the windows, the first three or four wholly mythical, the later ones approximating with increasing verisimilitude to the real people whom they represent, until one reaches the tenth, Michael John II himself, the patron of young Fischer, shown with amazing frankness as a Falstaffian figure of comedy, hand on hip, robes billowing round a portly body, laughing at the mock pomposity of his ancestors and the great hall which he had built to contain them. This is not a reverential place. The doors would more likely have been burst open by a crowd of revellers than by a well-ordered congregation. The statues prove it. They were by Tobias Kracker, who stood here in 1694 with Fischer von Erlach (we have an exact report of the occasion), to discuss what proved to be a brilliant collaboration between architect and sculptor. There is a sympathy of scale between the two artists which is matched by their sympathy of mood.

After the explosion of the Ancestors, the remainder of Vranov seems rather tame. Survivors among the mediaeval and Renaissance buildings are left to form the entrance, which passes promisingly over two viaducts and under curving archways to the inner courtyard. On the left is Fischer's chapel, a highly ingenious design of a circle surrounded by twelve ovals on two levels. In front is the main body of the house forming three sides to a courtyard. The evidence for dating these buildings is not very certain. Fischer von Erlach certainly drew up plans for the three wings,

OPPOSITE *The Ancestors' Hall, seen from its gallery. The ancestors of the Althans stand in niches between the lower windows. In the centre of the floor is a chess-board scaled for human chessmen. That the hall was not built for a solemn purpose is shown by the statue* ABOVE *of Michael John II of Althan, Fischer's patron, depicted by the sculptor, Tobias Kracker, 'with amazing frankness as a Falstaffian figure of comedy laughing at the mock pomposity of his ancestors and the great hall which he had built to contain them.'*

and one, the east, was built; but it seems that owing to the shortage of money, the south and west wings were not erected until the later part of the 18th century, and that in the interval the design was changed to a severer and duller Classicism. It is also unexplained why the pediment of the east wing should be out of centre. Some suggest that a north wing existed when the east was built, and that its later destruction produced the asymmetry. If that was so, it was an improvement, since the courtyard would have been dark and narrow if surrounded by buildings on all four sides, and the present view from the terrace of the courtyard is one of its two great attractions. The other is the pair of heroic statues, twice human size, which stand on each side of the outdoor stairway. They are by the Italian sculptor, Lorenzo Mattielli (1688-1740), and were originally commissioned by the Emperor Charles VI for Schönbrunn. He gave them to Maria Anna of Althan in about 1727, and the local tradition is that because they could only be dragged over the mountains from Vienna by snow-sledges, it

BELOW *The courtyard at Vranov. Facing is the east wing, the only one to be built to Fischer's design. In the centre is the external staircase which leads to the anteroom and thence to the domed Ancestors' Hall behind.*
OPPOSITE *One of the pair of heroic statues, Hercules struggling with Antaeus, which were originally made by Lorenzo Mattielli for the Austrian Emperor in about 1727, and brought to Vranov on snow-sledges shortly afterwards. They now stand against the balustrade of the external staircase.*

ABOVE *The oval hall, contained in the rectangular east wing, with its doors open to the Ancestors' Hall. These two rooms are the only ones at Vranov which retain their original 17th-century decoration. The remainder of the house was charmingly redecorated in the late 18th and early 19th centuries. In the sitting-room* OPPOSITE ABOVE, *known as the French salon, most of the furnishings came from France. The bedroom* RIGHT *is also French in feeling; one of the stoves is real, while the other opens like a door into a bathroom. In a corner of the library* LEFT *is one of the delightful landscapes which were added to the house in about 1787.*

was seven winters before they reached Vranov. Did anybody warn the Althans of their dimensions? They are completely out of scale with the rest of the façade, but so lively, so outrageous in this position, that they prepare the visitor for the equal defiance of convention immediately inside.

The Ancestors' Hall is linked to the rest of the house by another of Fischer's ovals, but none of his interior work survives in the main wings. Instead we have a set of rooms which were charmingly redecorated in the late 18th century and have remained untouched ever since. It is like moving from the hot room to the cool rooms of a Turkish bath to leave Fischer's stupendous hall for the ivory and gilt, the painted landscapes, the veiled bed-recesses and pattern-papered walls of this suite of rooms leading from it. Perhaps the lesson of Vranov is that while good decorative taste is always pleasing, it is but a feeble thing seen alongside the daring and triumph of great architecture carried indoors.

Gunterstein *Breukelen Holland c.1680*

Mediaeval builders in most countries had to choose between natural rock or an artificial moat for their defences. In Holland there was no choice, since there were no hills and superabundant water. Every house is still defended by a moat, at least on one side, for you can scarcely walk a hundred yards in Holland without striking water. How simple, then, for the builders of the first Gunterstein to open a sluice from the River Vecht and turn the site into an island. Of course, there were brick walls to hold the moat in place and bridges to cross it. But so universal is water that the moat appears not as a mediaeval curiosity around the house, but its natural element. With trees it is the opposite. There are lovely trees around Gunterstein, both on its immediate approaches and in the woods behind. But woods are no more natural to Holland than hedges. Perhaps there is not the space to spare. When they occur, as here, they give the landscape its much needed third dimension. If the moat defends Gunterstein, its trees screen it.

There has been a house here since the 14th century, and we know exactly what it looked like, since several drawings and at least one large painting of it survive. This is another happy peculiarity of Gunterstein. An exceptional amount is known about its history. The Dutch have not, on the whole, been very conscientious architectural historians. Their attitude towards houses is like our attitude towards people : to discover whether you like a person or not, you do not need to know all about his grandparents. But Gunterstein has remained in the same family ever since the 'new' house was built in the late 17th century, and its archives are correspondingly rich. Today it belongs to Jonker L. A. Quarles van Ufford, who has taken great pains to trace references to his house in the Utrecht archives and elsewhere. Hence the 'old' house is no mystery, although scarcely a brick of it survives. Its roots are in the present cellar ; its moat is the moat of the new house ; the names of its owners are known from generation to generation ; its appearance is shown in the painting which is reproduced on this page.

OPPOSITE *The entrance front, c.1680. There are two bridges over the moats, one from park to forecourt, the second from forecourt to house. On each side of the forecourt are the two detached wings which now form independent dwellings.* ABOVE *A painting of the old castle of Gunterstein, which is still in the house. The castle was destroyed in the French wars of 1673, but the present house was built on the same site and partly on its foundations.*

The castle was destroyed by the troops of Louis XIV when they retreated south towards Utrecht in September 1673. The destruction was almost complete; but the ruin found a remarkable purchaser in Magdalena Poulle, a French Huguenot born in Calais. In 1680, when she began to rebuild, she was a widow of nearly fifty, childless, but with a little nephew, Pieter Poulle, aged three, who laid the foundation stone – a stone, incidentally, which was discovered two hundred years later, when the moat was drained to inspect the foundations. Pieter died a few years after performing the only public function of his life. In the portrait of him, he holds the plan of the house in his hand.

Magdalena's architect was Adriaen Dortsman. The rebuilt Gunterstein was in many ways a most original house for Holland, and it would not be immediately identifiable as Dutch by someone only familiar with the tall gabled town-houses along the Amsterdam canals or the pretty spacious country-houses strung along both banks of the River Vecht. Among the Vecht houses Gunterstein stands out like a courtier among a flock of débutantes. It is not superficially pretty. It is masculine, still bearing some traces of its fortress origin. It is three-dimensional, with much architectural play between its different parts. Most of the canal houses, both in town and country, were built to make an immediate impact on the passer-by, like a row of court-cards dealt out side by side. Gunterstein has no main façade. Its entrance is almost apologetic – a porch pinched between two buttress-like wings – and the side of the house which it presents to the river and the public road is its back, an elevation devoid of architectural features except the windows and a semi-circular portico on two levels, an effective addition of 1823.

Two features of the exterior, however, excuse the architect from any charge of excessive modesty or plainness. In the centre of the high roof rises a little tower, which conceals the chimneys and an internal staircase by which the very top can be reached, and on each side of this tower, standing in a niche contrived in the thickness of the brick, is a white statue of one of the four seasons. This ingenious arrangement is also very charming. It lifts the whole house towards its apex and sets upon it the seal of good taste. It proclaims that Gunterstein is not a rebuilt castle but a finely designed house.

ABOVE *A closer view of the entrance, dated 1681 above the door.* TOP *A lovely feature of Gunterstein is the chimney-stack which also serves as a staircase-tower. Statues of the four seasons stand in niches round the outside.* OPPOSITE *The back of the house, which faces towards the public road but is effectively screened from it by trees. The pretty little portico at water-level and the balcony above it were added in 1823.*

TOP *The view from one side shows the relationship between the outlying wings, the bridge over the inner moat, and the main house. The nearer wing, once an orangery, but now converted into a dwelling for the owner of Gunterstein, conceals its pair which lies immediately behind.* ABOVE *The main room is lined with Gobelins tapestries specially woven for it in the late 17th century. Over the fireplace is the portrait of the builder, Magdalena Poulle, with her nephew Pieter, who laid the foundation stone in 1680 but died a few years later.* OPPOSITE *The entrance hall.*

The second feature is the arrangement of the approaches. There are two bridges over separate bands of water, and between them stands on each side a low pavilion which once contained the stables and an orangery, but which have now been converted into dwellings for the owner and a member of his staff. The pavilions are set back at the sides of the little courtyard allowing an unimpeded view of the entrance to the main house. Interest is thereby added to a façade which otherwise would appear brutally cramped. The architect tried to do too many things in his limited space on this façade, but in fairness to him it must be stated that the upper parts of the two 'wings' were added at the end of the 18th century. There is no fault to find, however, with the spatial relations of the pavilions. Whether seen from the entrance gates, from the river banks beyond, or from one of the upper windows of the house itself, they are delightful Dutch variants on the Palladian theme. Brick, water, whitened window-frames, cobbles, plants climbing trellises – these are some of the elements in a happy domestic picture : but it is the separation of the pavilions from each other and from the main house that gives it distinction and depth.

Inside there is a mixture of styles such as one would expect in a house occupied for three centuries by the same family. At no period was a clean sweep made of the past. Family portraits line the walls and large Dutch cupboards still stand in the corners for which they were presumably made. There is only one room furnished for show, and this contains not only the portrait of Magdalena with young Pieter, but a Gobelins tapestry round three of the walls, commissioned for the house and incorporating a view of the house as it was when newly built. The other rooms are comfortably domestic. Rippled light reflected from rippled water plays on the ceilings and the sides of polished cabinets. There is a room where the local water-control council meets, appropriately for a house which rises so confidently from land which would be waterlogged but for the superb skill and patience displayed by the Dutch in everything concerning hydraulics. Gunterstein may not be among the most beautiful houses illustrated in this book, but it does represent worthily that marriage between brick and water, and that decent cleanliness of building, which the Netherlands gave to the world.

Petworth House *Sussex England 1692-6*

ABOVE *The great house of the Duke of Somerset as it appeared in about 1700. The main block remains, but lacks the half-dome and the statues on the roof. Since this picture (now at Belvoir) was painted, the entrance was switched to the other side of the house, and the front-door became the park-door.* OPPOSITE *The façade of one of the terminal wings, seen on the left of the painting above. It is here that the French influence on Petworth's architecture is most evident.*

This is one of the very few great houses in England which is supposed to have been strongly influenced by French architecture. Horace Walpole could speak of it as being 'in the style of the Tuileries', and in our own times Sir John Summerson calls it 'conspicuously French' and Christopher Hussey 'a singular instance of French influence'. Except in the decoration of the centre and wings of the main façade, this influence is not now very apparent. To recapture its 'foreignness', one must look at the painting recently identified by Sir Anthony Blunt at Belvoir, showing the façade as it must have appeared soon after its completion in 1696. That this was not a fanciful reconstruction is proved by a very similar sketch which peeps out between the huge figures of Laguerre's wall-paintings on the Grand Staircase. Both show a balustrade surmounting a half-dome in the centre of the front. The balustrade is crowned by urns, and at the foot of the dome, on the parapet of the main roof-line, stand gesticulating statues, which are repeated on the parapets of the two wings. Ten further urns are spaced between the three groups. All this has now disappeared. It is supposed that a serious fire early in 1714 destroyed the dome and gutted much of the southern part of the house, and although the main fabric was soon rebuilt, the dome was not, and the statues and urns were lost for ever.

The main front of Petworth seen from across the lake. The roofline is flat, but the tower of the village church, which stands some way behind the house, occupies in this photograph approximately the position where the half-dome once broke the long expanse of roof.

By accident, therefore, Petworth was anglicised, and its only formal front simplified to the point of plainness. But it has three distinct characters – from the long, middle and short distance. You can see its full extent from over a mile away, across the lake, and from here it appears as a long grey house, its roof-line straight from end to end, punctuated only by regularly spaced chimneys. Its forty-two tall windows form two main floors. Its length and paleness are the first most obvious impressions. The second is its setting, for few parks curtsey so gracefully towards the house or cushion it so sympathetically. A rounded tree-covered knoll, partly artificial, dips from the north-west to flatten out at exactly the point where the podium of the house begins. The lake is serpentine, enlarged by Capability Brown between 1753 and 1763, and it is speckled with little islands on which stand great urns of stone or a single dripping willow. Its verge is neither marshy nor diked, but firmly drawn by low mossy banks, beyond which the uninterrupted parkland rises to the house, and herds of deer and sheep roam as far as the very windows.

On the nearer side of the lake, the park is mainly behind you and the details of the façade cannot yet be discerned. This therefore is its plainest aspect, and the point at which one most regrets the loss of the centrepiece. By chance one can replace it in imagination, for the blunted tower of Petworth church, which rises well behind the house, can be manoeuvred by walking to right or left to a position above the exact centre of the roof. One cannot, however, replace the gates and circular drive shown in the Belvoir picture, for the entrance was switched in the 19th century to the east side, between the church and the house, and from this distance there is nothing beyond the faint rustication of the three main bays and their scribbled decoration to indicate that the house has a focal point at all.

From the foot of the terrace or its pleasure-grounds to north and south the whole façade springs to life. Now one sees the variation of its stonework – rough, local stone for the main walls, Portland for the wings and centre, the firm surrounds for the doors and windows, the heavy cornice, the beautifully spaced balusters above it, the francophil busts and carvings above nine of the ground-floor windows, the subtle projection of the wings, the terrace and the stone seats along it. Look at either wing in isolation, and you will see that the attribution of French influence is justified and the charge of excessive plainness is not. All that is missing from a 'normal' house of the period, French or English, are giant pilasters in place of the modest rainwater pipes, and some emphasis for the central doorway.

Petworth, in proportion to its length and height, is a narrow house, only two rooms thick, and there was no space within it for the usual services. These are contained in loosely knit blocks behind and parallel to the main house, joined to it below ground by tunnels through which servants trundled food and fuel, and above ground by an archway constructed in the last century. The entrance drive now runs directly out of the little town of Petworth between those two blocks, and the whole building on this side is tightly belted in by a high wall dividing it from the busy streets immediately outside. This arrangement, odd for so patrician a house, has an historical origin. A nobleman's castle stood here since at least the 12th century, when it came into the possession of the great Percy family, later Earls of Northumberland, and it would have been normal for the town-houses to huddle close beneath the castle walls. It was several times rebuilt, but it kept its site and part of its massive structure. Some of the cellars of the present Petworth are semi-cylindrical caverns of near-Roman size and stubbornness, and the main walls of the chapel are those of the 13th century.

In 1682 Petworth passed by marriage from the Percies to the sixth Duke of Somerset, and it is to him, 'the Proud Duke', that we owe by far the larger part of the existing house.

He started rebuilding it with his wife's fortune in 1688. Basically its plan is simple. Nine state-rooms lead one into the other along the front facing the park, and are duplicated by rooms of similar size, but of lesser importance, behind. Some of them were refashioned after the fire of 1714 or in later centuries, adding thereby to the interest and continuity of Petworth's long history, but three of the most sumptuous remain as the Proud Duke created them at the end of the 17th century, and are of quite outstanding importance in the development of English art. These three are : the Marble Hall, the Grinling Gibbons Room, and the chapel.

The view of the same scene shown opposite, painted by J. M. W. Turner in about 1830. He was a constant visitor to Petworth.

The Marble Hall lies in the centre of the west front, and was the original entrance hall. Although it is strongly embellished, it is made to appear simple by its size, its lambency and its freedom from clutter. Its tones are white and pale green. In each wall there is a doorway. The centre one, opposite the glass park door, leads through a wide opening to the state dining room, with a Roman statue in a shadowed apse on each side of it. The floor is of green, black and white marble, and the ceiling plain. Two dove-grey fireplaces face each other from the north and south walls. All this gives the room its gossamer coolness, but its richness comes from the carving around the doors, above the fireplaces and along the cornice. There is nothing timid about this carving, all of which was the work of John Selden, the Duke's estate carver, who is not known to have worked elsewhere than at Petworth. To the 18th century it might have appeared gross. The egg and tongue moulding to the cornice, for example, and the acanthus brackets that project between it and the ceiling, are of unusual size, but they are delicate in their total impression because their scale is exactly right for the room. The framing round the doors and windows is broad and fluffy, like intertwined woollen fillets. The best of all are the surrounds of the fireplaces and the Duke's beasts, a bull and a unicorn, reclining above them on either side of his escutcheon. These splendid animals, angry in their precarious and unalterable positions, are carved in the round, but they are part of the architecture of the room, not ornaments placed around it. What a wonderful entrance it made!

The Marble Hall, originally the entrance hall of Petworth. It dates from the time of the Duke of Somerset, whose supporters, the bull and the unicorn, appear over the chimney-piece. The statue in the niche is Roman. OPPOSITE *The White and Gold Room in the private apartments of Petworth. The decorations were probably carried out in about 1770. The great mirror is Chippendale, and the chandelier is of 19th-century ormolu and Rockingham porcelain.*

ABOVE and BELOW *The Grinling Gibbons Room, Petworth's pride, and in Horace Walpole's opinion, the famous wood-carver's masterpiece. The carving is executed in limewood, and is a triumph of technique and delicate ingenuity. The portrait of Henry VIII after Holbein dominates the centre of the room, framed in Gibbons's carving, with a specimen of Jonathan Ritson's 'broochlike tracery' against the ceiling above.*

To the north, through the little dining room, lies Petworth's showpiece, the Grinling Gibbons Room. It does not arouse in the visitor the same immediate delight as many of the others, for its overall colour is parchment brown, and its proportions (sixty feet long by twenty-four wide and twenty high) are more those of a gallery than a room. Moreover, the burden of carving on the east wall is first seen from one end, and it consequently appears scabby in the mass. It is almost as if Grinling Gibbons, working at great pressure in his London studio (he was simultaneously busy on his designs for Hampton Court and the library at Trinity College, Cambridge), had concentrated on the individual carvings without considering carefully enough their total effect. Exquisite in detail, it is rather burdensome in bulk, in direct contrast to the Marble Hall, where the detail is heavy but the effect light. The panels behind the carvings were once painted white, but the paint was stripped off in about 1870 by Lord Leconfield. It was then thought an improvement, but the apparent greater delicacy of Jonathan Ritson's broochlike traceries against the white cove of the ceiling makes one wonder whether Gibbons' finer work would not benefit by the same background.

His scheme for the room was to supply three-sided frames for seven large portraits – a pair on each side of Henry VIII and a single portrait at either end of the room, as well as smaller pictures above the four doors. Each picture was surmounted by an immensely elaborate composition in carved limewood, from which depended drops or swags composed of flowers, game, fruit and objects which could be found in any gentleman's house. The light from the four west windows falls full on the main wall, but although one can see the lower parts of the drops clearly, the upper parts and the overpieces are placed too high for close inspection; yet photographs show that they were executed as carefully as if they could be seen at eye-level. Some of the carving is biscuit-thin, and in this single material Gibbons contrived with brilliant virtuosity the effect of every other – skin and feathers, shell and scales, leaf and petal, basketwork, violin strings, lace, the ribbon and metal of the Duke's coronet and Garter, the flesh of fruit and the flesh of cherubs' cheeks. Nothing is so dead as his dead birds, nothing so alive as his fluttering doves. Most of the carving is three-dimensional, but as the planes recede towards the wall, it is flattened to give the effect of even greater depth. Thus in flower-filled baskets, the ribs of the basket stand clear of the nearest flowers, while those behind are merely suggested by the point of a leaf, a half-hidden stem, but nothing seems crushed. The room is a museum of such artifices, and as such it should be studied, piece by piece.

In the chapel a glorious effect is achieved by placing late 17th-century gilded woodwork against 13th-century stone. The Early English arcades on each side are those of the Percies' chapel; the stalls, altar-rail, reredos, gallery and ceiling were added by the

Duke of Somerset in 1690-2. The floor of the chapel is eight steps below that of the main house, the gallery an equal height above it, and the variety of the walls and furnishings is made the more impressive by the changes in level. You look down upon the chapel before entering it, and then look up from the altar steps to the splendidly baroque proscenium of painted wood above the gallery. The huge east window is sparsely filled by armorial glass, and in daylight it is so dazzling that the magnolia outside the window is seen more clearly than the altar-piece within it. This is the only disturbing feature of a room which in its proportions, associations, ornament and muted colour is one of the most attractive in the house and the only one which frankly proclaims its ancient origins.

Among the later changes, one room in particular is a lovely example of its period. This is the White and Gold Room, a sitting-room in the private part of the house. It was redecorated in the late 18th century by Alicia Maria, Countess of Egremont, and is thought to be the room in Turner's *Drawing Room at Petworth*, now in the National Gallery in London. While its dimensions are not exactly those of a cube, it gives that satisfying impression. The basic colour of the panelled walls is faded ivory, against which are applied thin ribs and tendrils of gilded wood, nearer the rococo in style than Robert Adam, and as such rather an anachronism for their date. The 19th-century chandelier of ormolu and Rockingham porcelain is a beautiful piece of work, fully worthy of the Chippendale mirror above the fireplace, which must surely have been made for the room or the room for it. The third colour (after ivory and gilt) is the pale blue of the curtains, chair-coverings and flounces of the tables on each side of the fireplace ; and a fourth, the pinks of the carpet, a late 18th-century English design in the Aubusson manner. As a colour-scheme, and for its subtle mixture of style and period, this sitting-room is a wonderful composition : rich but private, delicate but ennobling.

Looking back on Petworth, one cannot escape the conclusion that it is a strange house. Its architecture, site and arrangements have a certain awkwardness. The confusion of the rooms on the east side of the main floor and of the bedrooms above it, together with the wanderings of the staircases and corridors between them, betray the lack of any thought-out plan, or the sacrifice of internal convenience to outside appearance on the west front and to historical chance on the east. Its architect, if there ever was one in the full sense, is unknown. But it contains rooms and a magnificent art-collection which are among the great glories of England. You can stand beside the picture which Turner, the favourite guest of the third Earl of Egremont, painted of its park in 1829, and by glancing out of the window see the same view which he captured so brilliantly on the canvas. Then, looking back along the receding vista of doors, you find yourself transplanted a further 140 years back to the days of the Proud Duke, whose patronage of artists left a legacy no less enduring.

The mediaeval chapel at Petworth was redecorated in the 1690s by the 6th Duke of Somerset, who added the plaster ceiling and the gallery over the entrance (ABOVE), *with its baroque, painted wooden drapery and coat-of-arms. The carvings were probably made by Selden in the early 18th century.*

On these two pages are the two separate parts of the building, the main house
RIGHT, and the stables (with wings for servants), BELOW. They confront
each other across the central forecourt which appears in both photographs, and
the relationship between them is clarified by the plan on the next page. The steps
to the stable and the decorative iron grill to the house were added later, and in
1914 the stables were converted into guest-rooms.

Buchlovice

Moravia Czechoslovakia 1700

If this delightful Italian villa were in Italy, it would be one of the best known and most visited houses in that country. As it lies in the centre of Czechoslovakia, near the battlefield of Austerlitz, its fame is less widespread than it deserves, although it welcomes some 100,000 visitors annually. Its special appeal is due to three things: the romantic circumstances of its building; the extraordinary charm and ingenuity of its design; and its garden-park of splendid exotic trees.

The house was built by an Italian for an Italian. Towards the end of the 17th century Agnes Eleonora Colonna married John Peterswaldsky, the inheritor of a fierce Moravian castle, Buchlov, which still stands on its hilltop a few miles away. As a condition of her engagement she stipulated (teasingly or with determination?) that she should not be obliged to live in the gothic discomfort of the ancestral home. She must have a new house built for her in the valley, and it must be in the Italian style. This expensive price for her hand was paid. Peterswaldsky commissioned an Italian architect, who is now thought to have been Domenico Martinelli, to design the new house. The main block was completed in 1701, and the stable-block some thirty years later. The familiar column, the badge of the Colonnas, appears everywhere alongside the peacock of the Peterswaldskies (which is represented here in flesh and feather as well as in paint and stone), and in the central panel of the domed saloon there is a painting of Agnes Eleonora receiving her house from a subservient muse. It is clear that her husband must have been very much in love with her.

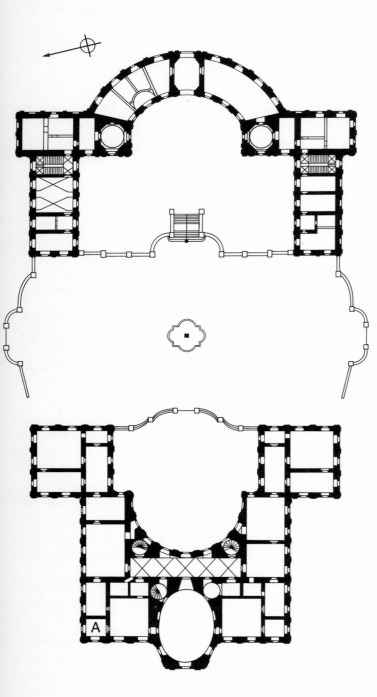

The main-floor plan of the stables (above) and the house (below). The oval room at the bottom of the house is the main hall under the central cupola. To the left of it, in the angle of the building, is the little room (A) where the Austrian and Russian Foreign Ministers met in 1908 for their historic conference.

The house is in two parts, like the separated halves of a broken cup. On the lower level we have the main living-house, and facing it the stable-block, which is given an architectural importance almost equal to that of the house itself. Each part is constructed as a semi-circular façade with wings, looking towards its counterpart opposite. The entrance-drive approaches the house through the gap. On the right, steps lead up to the stables ; on the left, we have the iron grill and gate to the front entrance. The visitor therefore finds himself turning from one building to the other, entranced by both individually and by their juxtaposition, but this pleasure cannot be conveyed photographically, for a hollow sphere cannot be photographed from within. One must be standing beside the central fountain to appreciate to the full the compliment which each of these buildings pays to the other. Formerly they were less distinct than they are today, since the iron grill and gate closing the forecourt of the house were added in about 1740, and the steps replaced a ramp in the early part of the present century when the stables were converted into separate suites for guests. We must therefore imagine that originally the carriage swept in direct from the highway round the semicircular court, and, when the passengers had alighted, the horses lugged the empty coach up the short steep ramp to the stables, where they and their coachmen and postillions took their refreshment in an architectural setting as splendid as the house itself.

The railings form a graceful addition with their double-curve and stone piers surmounted by vases and *putti*, but they slightly veil the main façade, which is an excellent example of the sculptural techniques of baroque architecture. The semicircle at the base of the court is a tight one, and its scale suggests that the house is smaller than it really is. There is a considerable amount of decoration on this façade ; the capitals to the pilasters, for instance, cluster together at the corners with the fecundity of baskets of fruit, and the balustrade along the roofline is topped by stone urns beautifully spaced. Behind it is the cupola of the central hall, rising above the whole group with queenly self-assertiveness. It is the sort of view which makes one immediately eager to go inside and discover how this curving façade has been adapted internally.

But before doing so, we must walk round the house and discover its other dimension. The natural slope of the ground has been used to transform an apparent one-storey pavilion into a house with two clearly defined floors, and the central cupola, which from in front appeared to be little more than an elegant capping to a main room, is seen from behind to be the roof of a large octagonal tower. Exterior steps lead down through the garden to connect the upper level with the lower. The effect of this arrangement is wholly delightful. It joins house to garden, and it doubles the size of the house unobtrusively. The way in which the transition is made repays careful study. At no point is there any awkwardness, for the proportions of dome, balustrade, windows and pilasters have been calculated with great care to suit both a one-storey and two-storey building.

Of the two floors, the upper one was reserved for the family and guests and the floor below for the services. There is only one

RIGHT *Agnes Eleonora Colonna, for whom Buch-*
lovice was built in about 1700. A portrait in the
house. BELOW *A closer view of the entrance. The*
peacock is alive, but it is also found painted and
sculptured in many parts of the house as the family
badge of the Peterswaldskies.

ABOVE *The big oval saloon or ballroom, now used for local weddings, rises to the full height of the cupola and is ringed by a gallery at mid-elevation. The stucco is attributed to an Italian, Balthasar Fontana (1658-1736). The Peterswaldsky peacock reappears in the shield on the right.*

ABOVE RIGHT *The 'sala terrena', or summer dining-room, at the lower garden level of Buchlovice. The fountain and stuccoed ceiling are by Italian artists. In hot weather water was sprinkled on the pebbled floor to cool the room by its gradual evaporation.*

OPPOSITE *The central corridor, between the fore-court and the big saloon, which greatly simplifies the internal circulation of the house.*

exception to this : on the lower floor a *sala terrena*, or summer dining-room, has been made with a shallow-domed ceiling, walls of mosaic and a pebble floor on which water would be sprinkled to cool the room in hot weather. At one end of it is a fountain. The room also introduces the stucco of the house, which was probably executed by Balthasar Fontana in about 1710. It is provincial stucco, lacking the graces of a Benrath or Ludwigsburg illustrated elsewhere in this volume, but flowing with an easy uninhibited line, and adding to the usual classical or religious themes, scenes of the stuccoist's own invention. Stucco of this kind will be found throughout the house, particularly on ceilings, but also blending with stone to form the surrounds of doors and windows.

All the other family and guest-rooms occupy the first floor on a level with the *cour d'honneur*. The rooms lead one into the next, but always with an escape-route into a corridor or the big saloon or into the court itself. They vary in size, but only in the case of the saloon do they vary in height. This house could illustrate the

LEFT *A view from the corner-room (A on the plan) which was the scene of the meeting between Aehrenthal and Iswolski at Buchlovice in 1908.*
BELOW *The dining-room, with a tiny chapel opening out of it. The portrait is of John Peterswaldsky, builder of Buchlovice. The chandelier is Venetian.*

absurdity of the contention that big rooms must have high ceilings and small rooms low ceilings, for any awkwardness in the proportions has been disguised by the clever use of curves and interior decoration. They are very habitable rooms. The furniture has been left very much as it was before the last war. It is the accumulation of several centuries, and it still has the atmosphere of a private house, though it is now the property of the State. Its character is that of a well-endowed family of the last years of the Austro-Hungarian Empire. Some of the best furniture was made locally at different periods; other pieces were imported from Vienna or France. The succession of family portraits, the gradual collection of the library, ends with 1945, but although the social climate has changed, a respect for the tradition remains.

One room in particular reminds us of a vanished age. Buchlovice had passed by marriage from the Peterswaldskies to the Berchtolds in about 1800. In 1908, when Count Berchtold was Austrian Ambassador in St Petersburg, he offered his house as a quiet retreat where the Austrian and Russian Foreign Ministers, Aehrenthal and Iswolski, might meet to discuss the Balkan question. They met in this tiny angle-room on 16th October, and from their discussion arose the agreement that Austria might annex the Slav provinces of Bosnia and Herzegovina in return for Austrian agreement to Russia's penetration of the Turkish straits. How strange it is to contemplate that the consequence of this historic agreement was to shatter the peace in which it was conceived! There would have been a First World War even if the Buchlovice meeting had never taken place; but by chance things were said in this little cabinet which made it inevitable.

A bedroom on the main floor (where all the family bedrooms were situated), with a wide canopy over the brass bedstead. The whole house, though now the property of the State and uninhabited, is still furnished very much as it was in the 18th and 19th centuries.

Already by 1908 the house was surrounded by the present park, and the increasing maturity of the trees has made it one of the loveliest small parks in Europe. The trees were collected from many parts of the world by two famous botanists, Leopold Berchtold (1759-1809) and his brother-in-law Frederick (1781-1876), the co-founder of the Czech National Museum in Prague. The layout of the garden, including the central basin, had been completed in the mid-18th century by the son of the builder of the house, and we now see the successful mingling of two traditions in garden-architecture, the classical-baroque and the 'English', improved by the high quality of the decorative trees and the excellent condition in which the park is still maintained. It is on a large scale. You can get temporarily lost among the winding paths, and the trees, which as saplings must have looked lost in the big garden-architecture, now rival the house in height and brush against its upper walls. What a place, one thinks, to return to! How deeply must this house and garden have been loved! It contains so much of the best of old Europe, in taste, in imagination and in quality, that it is good to find that the new Europe appreciates these things as much in the East as in the West.

BELOW *The side of the house as it dips towards the garden. The exotic trees, which have made the garden as famous as the house, were collected by two distinguished members of the Berchtold family, who came into possession of Buchlovice in about 1800.*

OPPOSITE *The garden front. The fountain in the foreground, with its putti playing musical instruments, was erected in the mid-18th century by Sigismund Charles Peterswaldsky, son of the builder. On this side, the house is given an extra storey by the fall of the ground, converting the central cupola into a tower.*

Schloss Ludwigsburg

Württemberg Germany 1704-33

Only a small part of this glorious palace is described and illustrated in these few pages, since to describe it all would be to overwhelm its neighbours. But the part selected is a self-contained unit, the first section of the whole complex to be built, and contains in its dozen rooms some of the best secular baroque that Germany can offer.

The Schloss Ludwigsburg took thirty years to build, 1704-33, to the designs first of Johan Friedrich Nette, and after his death in 1714, of the Italian architect Donato Frisoni. It was built for the Duke Eberhard Ludwig of Württemberg as a palace not of regal, but of imperial, size, since with its park, vistas and attendant country-houses it embraces a huge area between Stuttgart and the town of Ludwigsburg ten miles away. The main courtyard of the palace is large enough to parade an entire infantry-division, and the pavilions and *corps-de-logis* which form it would separately count as considerable palaces for half-a-dozen less splendid courts. This grandiloquent building is also very beautiful. In summer its golden stone is shadowed like a hundred sundials by the exquisite mouldings round the doors and windows, and, as the accompanying photographs of the exterior clearly show, it is a

ABOVE *An engraving of the palace from the south made in 1709. The central block, the 'Old Corps-de-Logis', was built first, soon followed by the two buildings at right-angles to it. The arcades on each side of the Corps-de-Logis were then glassed-in to form galleries leading to pavilions at either end. This part of the work was finished by Donato Frisoni in 1717.* OPPOSITE *The south front of Schloss Ludwigsburg. The private rooms of the Duke of Württemberg, in which all the interior photographs on these pages were taken, lie along the first floor. The roof, shown in its original form above, was later heightened to incorporate an attic storey.*

beautifully proportioned building on both its main fronts. The part with which we are concerned is the Old *Corps-de-Logis* or *Fürstenbau* which closes the north side of the courtyard, and the two wings that project in line with it to east and west. The south side overlooks the courtyard, the north side drops away to the park. The whole of this group was built between 1704 and 1717, the central block first, by Nette, followed by the wings to Nette's designs executed by Frisoni. The upper storey and mansard roof with its lantern were added at a still later date.

More particularly we are concerned with the first floor of the building, where the Duke had his private apartments. These consisted of five rooms in the central block, and two terminal pavilions connected by galleries to the main building. You can see through the open doors from end to end. The rooms are not very large, but each of them was beautifully finished in the taste of the early-18th century by stuccoists, woodworkers and painters who wandered from court to court in Germany as once they had in Italy and France. The rooms are maintained today by the *Land* of Württemberg in perfect condition. Wisely they are unencumbered by furniture beyond a few exquisite pieces, mostly French, some tapestries and a few portraits on the walls. The furniture of the rooms is their decoration – in all three dimensions and in every known form of the decorator's art except metal.

The most conventional are the rooms in the centre, which are darkened by fine woods and tapestries and are devoid of stucco. This suite separates the two side wings which give access to the pavilions – the game-room at the east end and the hunting-room

at the other. The game-room is one of the most delightfully ingenious rooms of the century. It is basically rectangular, occupying the whole of the first floor of a square pavilion, but its ceiling
has been formed into a painted dome and its corners cut diagonally to make four little separate rooms in which the Duke and his
visitors could play cards or board-games in seclusion. The pavilion therefore has the shape of a small octagonal basilica with
attendant chapels leading off it. The problems created, and the
solutions found to them, are there for all to see. It is beautifully
designed and constructed. Once the shapes were settled, they
were embellished charmingly. The colour is cream and pink and
white – a rich parquet on the floor, kicking *putti* on the cornice, a
chandelier hung centrally like a bag of glass, and uncomplaining
demi-gods holding up parts of the roof.

The pair to it, the *Jagdpavillion*, (so-called for no other reason
than that there are a few hunting emblems scattered around,
and that the gentlemen of the court repaired here after the chase)
is less inventively sub-divided but even more lavishly embellished. About half the space is taken up by a single room of great
richness, and the remaining half partitioned into three cabinets.
One of these is a Chinese lacquer closet; a second an extra-
ordinarily careful design of coloured woods which cover every
square inch of the floor, walls and ceilings, as if it were not a room
but a box. How could it have been used? Not surely by hunters to
remove their boots? It could not have contained a single piece of
furniture, for it is furniture itself, a thing to admire, a luxury toy of
infinite elaboration and skill.

ABOVE *The central rooms of the Duke's suite at
Ludwigsburg are decorated and furnished to the
highest possible standards of the early 18th century,
including several French pieces, like this beautiful
Louis XV commode.* ABOVE LEFT *The five inner
rooms lead at each end into narrow galleries, which
lead in turn to the two pavilions. This is the inner end
of the west gallery, with sculptures of Fame (left)
and Kingship by Diego Carlone.* OPPOSITE *The
Spielpavillon, or game-room, in the east wing, looking down the full length of the floor towards the Jagd
or Hunting pavilion. Two of the four little card-
playing rooms are glimpsed right and left of the
door. The wall decorations and ceiling-painting (the
latter by Luca Aurelio Colomba) are superb examples
of the late baroque.*

TOP *The mirror-room, or 'cabinet d'amour', finished in 1716, leads off the Duke's bedroom at
Ludwigsburg. Its numerous mirrors, of all shapes
and sizes and set at all angles, were presumably designed to heighten his sensuous pleasures.* ABOVE *A
pair of Turkish prisoners, by Diego Carlone, in the
east gallery.* OPPOSITE *The Chinese lacquer cabinet
in one of the four small rooms in the* Jagdpavillon.
*Fantastic birds and dragons in chinoiserie blend
perfectly with the exquisite parquet of the floor.*

A third room, opening off the Duke's bedroom, was even
stranger in appearance but more explicable in intent. This was
his 'mirror-room' – a euphemism for a *cabinet d'amour*, which he
copied for his pleasure from late-17th-century Dutch originals.
Mirrors of different shapes are set in great profusion and at
different angles on the walls and ceiling, while the other decorations are mainly nude bas-reliefs in heavy gold, as crude in
execution as in purpose. The room with its oriental lasciviousness
strikes the only false note in the palace.

Compare to it the treatment of the sculptures by Diego
Carlone in the two galleries adjoining. Here there is just as much
writhing flesh, and on ten times the scale; but at no point does its
voluptuousness nauseate. These lovely baroque statues have a
controlled sensuality, whether they be playful goddesses in the
round, or quick sketches of Ovidean scenes dashed off in stucco.
They are human figures caught in mid-gesture, just as their
swinging draperies stand out stiffly in folds which gravity would
alter in a split-second. Here is the baroque equivalent of the
candid camera-shot – true representations of sudden attitudes
and emotions, more revealing of personality than portraits posed.
In the eastern gallery the life-size stucco figures are of Turkish
prisoners-of-war. Are they miserable? Some are; while others
talk urgently to their manacled partners. But had they all worn
expressions of uttermost agony, they would still have given the
pleasure which they did not feel themselves.

186

Villa Agnelli *Piedmont Italy c.1715*

The road from Turin leads towards the Alps past the stupendous palace of Stupinigi, which the Sicilian architect Juvarra built for Victor Amadeus II, Duke of Savoy and King of Sicily and Sardinia. The palace was called a hunting lodge, but it contains one of the most flamboyant baroque ballrooms in the world. When we learn that the Villa Agnelli, some twenty miles further on, was built as another hunting-lodge by the same architect for the same patron, we never expect to find something so comparatively modest or so exquisitely tender. The attribution to Juvarra is based on some drawings for the staircase and long gallery in his hand, and certain similarities between this house and his Palazzo Madama in Turin. It is also known that he built the church which still stands alongside it. That Victor Amadeus was the first owner is also probable, since there is a record that the land belonged to the house of Savoy until 1740. The presumption therefore is that the Villa Agnelli began its existence as a royal retreat designed by the great architect who enriched Piedmont with so many buildings at the start of the 18th century. The church is dated 1716, and the Villa Agnelli could be almost contemporary.

It lies just below the domed church on a saddle of land between two streams. One of them is the river Chisone, which cleaves a passage through the mountains to the French frontier, some thirty miles away by road. The other, infinitely more modest, is a mountain stream which runs impatiently through the garden. Snow-peaks close the horizon to the north, and all around are steep pine-covered slopes and little chalets and farmhouses which vary quixotically in their homespun architecture between Tuscan and Alpine. The air is sharp and clear. The church-bells toll solemnly every quarter-hour, with that hollow note which all bells acquire in mountains, whether hung in steeples or from the necks of cows. The grass is very green, and the trees, with which the villa's surroundings are profusely endowed, are in springtime diaphanously fresh and luminous. Clearly, whatever purposes the villa may once have served for the chase, today it is the perfect refuge from the heat of the great plain around Turin.

ABOVE *The entrance front. It is not very large or sumptuous for an originally royal palace, and in restoring it, the present generation of the Agnelli family have kept its air of aristocratic simplicity.* OPPOSITE *Juvarra's domed church at Villar Perosa, dated 1716, stands above the house, to which it is connected by terracing.*

The approach to the villa is between sloping lawns which reveal its creamy walls by degrees. There is restrained swagger about the entrance façade in the voluted pediments on the roofline and little balustrades along the first-floor windows. It does not clearly proclaim itself as Italian, except perhaps by the large diamond-shaped stone tiles of the roof, and it might pass as a villa of distinction almost anywhere along the Riviera. It is a surprise to find such a building in the mountains, but this is because it is a rare survivor among the many villas which were constructed here in the 17th and 18th centuries, only to be destroyed in the frontier wars with France. (The Villa Agnelli itself was hit by two bombs in 1943, fortunately without causing irreparable damage, for it is strongly built of stone.) The garden façade is more generously designed with two superimposed rows of open arches, behind which are upper and lower loggias, which strengthen the impression that the villa was a summer resort.

The French have an architectural term '*maison de lanterne*', which well expresses the character of the villa. It is not a lantern in the sense of being open on all sides, for many of its rooms are intimate and some rather dark. But it is a house of many apertures, and in walking through it you find yourself either half out-of-doors in the loggias or between great windows, like those of the main staircase, which suspend you as airily as bird-cages.

This staircase, and the hall which leads to it, occupy the whole central bay of the house on the entrance side, and it is of a simple magnificence which reinforces the claim to a royal origin and prepares you for the surprise of the interior. The Villa Agnelli is neither grand nor sumptuous, for its great elegance is achieved by the clever use of inexpensive materials. Piedmont, when it achieved its independence under Victor Amadeus, was impoverished by war, and even the King could not afford silks and marbles. The treads and banister-rail of the staircase, for instance, are of local stone, but the balusters are of pottery, and ring, when struck by the finger-nail, each with a different note. The staircase rises in double flights to join at a landing on the first floor – again in the grand tradition, but you immediately notice that the wall decorations are of lightly fashioned stucco and create the effects of delicacy and playfulness at minimum cost. It is almost as if the design had been left to the imagination of the stuccoist, for tricks are played with the classical orders (a Corinthian capital split open to admit a basket of flowers) which no 'serious' architect would have permitted but which are utterly delightful.

The head of the staircase opens into the long gallery. It is unfortunate that the stair-block should darken this lovely room along the greater part of its length, for it should be seen in all its gentle colours and consistently illuminated from end to end. This is its only fault. A gallery is an awkward shape for decoration and furnishing, and never has the problem been more successfully overcome than here. The wall facing the windows is divided by nine identical doorways leading to the inner rooms, each surmounted by a pelmet and framed with an easy grace which again breaks all the rules of classical symmetry. The ceiling, if flat or barrel-vaulted, would have been too rigid; instead, it is vaulted

ABOVE *Between the gallery and the upper loggia of the Villa Agnelli are five small sitting-rooms, with curtains between them instead of doors, giving the effect of connected pavilions. In the nearer room the Chinese wallpaper is original, and the whole suite is decorated in the 'Barochetto' style, half-baroque, half-rococo, of the early 18th century.* OPPOSITE *The upper loggia opens off a series of small rooms, some of which are decorated with Chinese wallpaper and refurnished in the same spirit.* BELOW *Two majolica vases on each side of a Chinese monkey.*

with a free, rolling gait that strikes exactly the right compromise between informality and sophistication. From it hang four chandeliers decked out with ribbons and metal ivy-leaves, and all the way down each side are wall-brackets holding pairs of candles. How beautiful the room must look when they are lit!

But all this is but the framework for the *chinoiserie* paintings on the walls. The early 18th century was the heyday of the Chinese fashion throughout most of Europe, and Piedmont was particularly exposed to it by oriental imports through Genoa. The original *carte alla cinese* were too expensive for use in quantity, but Piedmontese painters soon became adept copyists of the style, and each one of these delightful paintings is a brilliant example of it. Against pale blue backgrounds scenes of Chinese life are painted with a perfect understanding of those courteous, apologetic gestures adopted by the Chinese (at least in art) in their most humdrum activities; and rising above the human figures are slim branching trees, flowering but leafless and apparently rootless, and extending upwards as far as the panel demanded. The paintings are framed and prolonged by coloured stucco which thins out towards the ceiling to give the effect of a pergola. All is mixed – Chinese and Italian; paint and stucco; *trompe l'œil* and reality. But colour and style are consistent throughout – that early toying with rococo when it was freshest and least self-conscious. The craftsman who added in a couple of minutes a twirl of plaster here, an extra spray of roses there, was only suiting his own taste and eye, but the product of his simple fancy has continued to give pleasure for centuries.

The other rooms on the main floor lie between the long gallery and the loggia, and have no true outside windows except at each end. Having to borrow their light, they are cool and secluded, and none of them is very large. Once they were bedrooms, with bathrooms formed from the loggia, but now five of them are sitting-rooms, some opening into the others through tent-like curtains instead of doors, and all with easy access to the gallery and the loggia, which has now been reopened to its full length. The layout is unusual, but apart from the minor inconvenience of providing no room in which more than a dozen people can meet, it is very pleasant, for it invites at the same time intimacy and variety, and the long loggias above and below serve the same purpose as the sheltered decks of a ship opening off the cabins. You can walk there and you can sit there, enjoying the view, while chandeliers sway slightly above you in the breeze.

All these rooms follow the *Barochetto* (half-baroque, half-rococo) style of the hall and gallery. One room has some of the original Chinese wallpaper, patterned with exotic birds and fruit, and the ceilings are all coved and painted in sympathetic colours and designs. The furniture, too, matches perfectly. It is mostly Piedmontese, with some Genoese, of the 18th century, simple, almost rustic, in design, copying the main lines of contemporary French furniture but replacing veneer or ormolu by paint and stucco – peasant furniture, you might conclude, like that of Provence, to which it bears a marked resemblance, were it not for its certainty of taste and modest elegance which have

Giovanni Agnelli's bedroom contains this magnificent bed, with bedhead and linen hangings embroidered in coloured wools, a style peculiar to Piedmont and known as bandera. It follows the same general rococo designs which are executed in paint and stucco elsewhere in the house. RIGHT The lower of the two loggias, in which cane furniture and rush matting blend harmoniously with the simple arcading of the loggia and the staircase curving to the loggia above.

made these pieces collectors' prizes. The embroidery, on chairs and bedcovers, is also distinctively Piedmontese, known as *bandera,* where coloured wools are stitched on a background of linen, producing an effect of delicious softness both in texture and in tone. There is not an ugly object in this house. Although some of its contents could have come from a cottage, they sit happily alongside works of art. An effect of luxury is produced by methods so unerudite that it is difficult to understand how it was done, even though every separate part of it can be explained.

Outside there is a garden leading by terraces and shelving lawns to the stream. The terraces are 19th-century and excellent of their kind, but the water-garden has only been created during the last ten years to the designs of Russell Page. Every garden is a taming and refinement of nature : this garden has transplanted a piece of England to the Italian Alps. The stream has been broadened at intervals into pools, connected by waterfalls and cotton-thread rivulets of running water, and is surrounded by trees and flowering shrubs. Within a fairly small space there is drama, repose, level ground and strong contour, broken colour and plain green. A bridge crosses a miniature gorge, a cherry avenue is discovered dripping petals like confetti, and there is a sound of wind in the treetops while all remains calm below. Looking upwards you see a corner of the house and the half-cheek of one of the domes of Juvarra's church.

The Villa Agnelli is called after a famous Italian family, who still inhabit it during occasional holidays and the late summer months. It was first acquired by an Agnelli, a cavalry officer, in about 1813. His grandson, who was born in the house, was the founder of the Fiat car-manufacturing company, and Giovanni Agnelli, grandson of the founder and present head of Fiat, is now the owner of the villa. With all their many other properties and interests, it occupies a very special place in the family's affections, and the care and taste with which Signora Agnelli has restored it after the damage done in the last war have not only saved for Italy a house of exceptional interest, but have created an atmosphere within it and around it which is among the most perfect described in this book.

The garden front of the Villa Agnelli is the more original of the two, being formed of two superimposed loggias which run almost its entire length. These form connecting corridors for the rooms behind as well as cool places in which to sit. The upper storey was added at the end of the 19th century for guest rooms.

Schloss Schönborn *Stockerau Austria 1712-17*

The country between Vienna and the north-eastern borders of Austria is useful more than attractive. Huge fields of ripening corn roll solemnly for miles. The farms are grouped in villages and the churches are red and sturdy. Suddenly you come across a wholly unexpected monument standing at a corn-field's edge, a shrine to St John, who raises his haloed head to the stone canopy, pierced for his better view of heaven. The statue and its frame are Austrian baroque of the first quality, and instinctively you look around for the great house or monastery to which it must have been attached. You find Schönborn. But it is barely visible from this point, although only a quarter of a mile away. It hides its secrets behind a park and a network of small lanes. It has no view except of the immediate alleys through the woods. When you first see the full extent of the house, it is through its orangery, and the first impression is one of beckoning statues and swirling stone.

Schönborn was built in 1712-17 for the family of the same name by Lukas von Hildebrandt. He was known above all for his 'brilliant spatial interlocking and fiery decoration' (Nikolaus Pevsner), and already from this first vista both can be recognised. The orangery, in effect, is a sort of introduction to the house, gesturing the visitor towards it, both opening and confining the view, and with its two curved wings setting the rhythms of alternating recession and advance which will be maintained throughout. The orangery is about 500 yards from the house, providing a view from the main windows close enough to be interesting, but far enough away to avoid a sense of enclosure. As you walk up the avenue, the 'fiery decoration' becomes clearer.

The entrance porch of Schönborn is a beautiful work of art, both in structure and in detail. Although the house is masterful and symmetrical, Hildebrandt's use of sculpture and surface decoration has given it a carefree elegance, like a pianist who with one hand sounds the deeper themes and with the other provides a running commentary. The baroque statues on the roofline, formal in their siting, could not be less formal in their postures – arguing, applauding, striking attitudes of astonishment or

The shrine to St John, outside the park. OPPOSITE *The entrance front. Sculpture and surface decoration give the symmetrical house 'a carefree elegance.'*

disdain. Their waving hands and billowing drapery express an exuberance which is the character of the whole house. Below, a pediment outlined by graceful brackets contains the coat of arms of the Schönborns, a superb coroneted shield flanked by two sulky lions. Then come three windows with decorated arches, and a balcony railed in iron with stone supports to two lanterns at the corners. The whole is supported on four slim Corinthian columns forming a shelter for arriving carriages. It is immensely sure and boldly free.

Behind, the house opens up more widely than one expects with two wings prolonging the side-façades, and two further wings standing at right-angles to them, the whole forming the pattern of the capital Greek letter Omega (Ω). The hollow is a courtyard at the back. In none of these other façades did Hildebrandt express himself quite so vigorously as on the front. There are stuccoed surrounds to the windows in the shape of cartouches or ovals, and the right-angle where one wing turns into the other is ingeniously softened by inserting a turret-staircase. A clock-tower, dominant as a church-steeple, rises above a further court-yard where the stables and other services are found. Around the whole complex of this large country-house extends the park.

The first view of Schönborn is from the orangery, which repeats more modestly the statues, green shutters and curling stone of the main house. The intervening ground is now left fairly rough, but in the 18th-century view (ABOVE) there was a formal garden with a long central canal. RIGHT 'The baroque statues on the roofline, formal in their siting, could not be less formal in their postures.'

The park is one of the most exciting features of Schönborn. It is not very large – you could walk right round it in an hour – but it contains a great variety of natural and artificial ornament which in its present full maturity is at the same time splendid and rather sad. On the shores of the central lake is a circular classical temple, ringed by the rustication of its masonry, dappled by the shadows of surrounding trees, domed, painted internally in a Pompeiian manner, and expressing all the melancholic admiration for the classical past which affected the European aristocracy in the mid-18th century from Stourhead to Leningrad. Above the door the metal letters APOLLINI SACRUM have been wrenched out, but their impression is still legible. In another part of the park, we have its oriental reflection, a little Chinese kiosk on an island linked to the lake-shore by a bridge of simple ironwork. These pretty buildings do not occupy prominent positions. They end no vistas, and are chance discoveries rather than the objects of a walk. They were temples for reflection or picnics.

Unhappily the interior of Schönborn was a partial victim of the last war. In 1945 a Soviet battalion was billeted there for some six months, and no house created for the leisured and cultured few can survive for long occupation by the uncaring many. Much of the furniture and other works of art was destroyed. But the main hall with its stuccoed pairs of herms survives almost intact, and there is a pleasant staircase behind, though modest for a house of such importance. The main reception rooms on the first floor were remodelled in the 19th century and are almost bare of furniture. The chapel, however, still contains its original stucco and ceiling-paintings, and is a room of interesting proportions, tall and narrow, with the family's pew entered from the first floor facing the altar from high above.

Schönborn is one of the masterpieces of the high period of Austrian baroque. Today it bears the scars of its ill-treatment, and within the last decade it was further damaged by a flood which filled the ground floor with water to a depth of three feet. But the main façade and the park were almost unaffected by these disasters, and the grace, vivacity and elegance of Hildebrandt are still there to be enjoyed.

Solar Mateus *Vila Real Portugal 1725-35*

The house is a little too rustic to be called a palace, and a little too grand to be called a villa. The word *solar* in Portuguese can best be translated as *château*. There is no exact English equivalent. 'Manor-house' suggests something too stable and conventional for this extravaganza, but it is otherwise apt, since the house was built as the centre of an agricultural estate as well as a nobleman's country residence, and its earthiness is as important as its aristocratic daring. For a building so rooted to the soil, it is astonishingly original. It is true that in the architecture of neighbouring villages one can see something of the swirl and exclamatory flourish of Mateus; but this form of Portuguese baroque was usually reserved for churches, and Mateus rises from its vineyards in startling contrast to its neighbours. There are very few private houses of its size in Portugal, and none of its distinctiveness. It makes no use, inside or out, of that most characteristic form of Portuguese decoration, the *azulejo* tile. Its character was given to it by an Italian, yet nothing like this is to be found in Italy. It is very Portuguese, but very much itself.

Its history is not fully documented, but one can safely assume that is was begun in about 1725 for Antonio Mourão, and that during the course of its building, the façade was added by Nicoló Nasoni, who emigrated from Florence to Oporto in 1731 and became Portugal's leading baroque architect. The adjoining chapel, in the same style, was consecrated in 1759, and may be by one of Nasoni's pupils. The house and chapel have remained virtually unchanged since they were built, and have never passed by sale out of the original family. The present owner is the Count of Mangualde, whose mother was a Mourão.

The house lies near Vila Real in northern Portugal, among the vineyards which produce the Mateus rosé wine, and at the foot of the Serra do Marao range, which rises to a height of 4,600 feet. The entrance front (OPPOSITE) was probably designed by the Italian architect Nasoni in the 1730s, and the baroque chapel to its left added in the 1750s by one of his pupils. The garden front is seen ABOVE, with the chapel on the right. Below is the huge yew-tunnel.

The appearance of the house is familiar all over the world from the label on bottles of Mateus rosé wine, which is manufactured close by from vines grown on the estate. On the far side of a square pond two wings advance hospitably to enclose a courtyard, at the far end of which is a double flight of stairs leading to a central door on the first floor. A fairly conventional arrangement. But to this is added baroque detail of such outrageous, such outlandish, size and swagger that the house loses all its feudal dignity and becomes a phenomenon. Finials almost as tall as the house itself rise from the corners of the roof, as bulbous as chessmen, as emphatic as exclamation-marks, and give it an air of amused surprise. Between the finials is mounted a further battery of ornamentation. The outside staircase is a decorative encrustation, and the windows are surmounted by shells and scrolls which flow as easily in stone as if they were made of ribbon. Above this again is a balustrade which lifts at the centre to introduce the coat-of-arms of the family, executed with immense *brio*, the supporting lions rolling back their heads and swishing their tails in uproarious delight. Finally we have two statues, feathered warriors, male and Amazon, pricking the skyline with their spears, the sculptural equivalent of the contorted figures which were so often painted on the domed ceilings of baroque ballrooms.

ABOVE *The topiary garden behind the house was laid out in 1933. The colour of the walls is basically white, with ornamentation in an ochre stone.*
OPPOSITE *A closer view of the entrance with its brilliant baroque embellishments. The stable doors are on the courtyard level, and the door to the main salon at the top of the outside staircase. The arms of the builder, Antonio Mourão, are above it.*

TOP *The old stables, which lie immediately below the main reception room of the house. They are not used for horses, but the heavy stone mangers and the floor of flag-stones and cobbles remain exactly as built.*
ABOVE *The centre of the house contains this open courtyard, from which one mounted by elaborate external staircases to the main floor. The ground floor was entirely reserved for the servicing of the house and its estate, and it was possible to drive through the courtyard from the front of the house to the back.*

It is not absurd. It is the house of a laughing cavalier. It is witty and jovial and endearing. It is not very good architecture. All the rules are broken. The pediments of the windows, for example, have ceased to serve the purpose of keeping off the rain, for they are overhung by the wide cornice of the roof, and are mere decoration, like painted eyebrows. In the composition of the façade, no scheme can have been carefully drawn out beforehand. Lumps of stone carving were applied where there was room to fit them as icing might be added to a cake. Yet if there is no certainty of design, there is a certainty of intention and a unity of mood. It stands, without irreverence, alongside its chapel, each expressing in stone an outlook on life and religion which is both masterful and jolly.

On the ground level is all the apparatus of a country estate. It is difficult to separate what was intended for the running of the house from what was intended for the farm. But, on the whole, the ground floor was rustic and the first floor noble. On descending from your carriage at the foot of the main steps, you mounted to the hall while the horses were led into the stable immediately beneath it. The sounds and smells of equine refreshment mingled with human. Beyond the stables, in the centre of the house, is an enclosed court, overlooked by the bedrooms and dining room. This was often occupied by pigs, chased by scullions from the kitchen, as can be seen from some 19th-century drawings of Mateus preserved in the house. There must have been a constant clatter, an immense coming and going of peasants and overseers, a bustle and a *bonhomie* which did not accord ill with what we know of the generous and flamboyant characters of the Mourãos, many of whom rose high in the service of the arts and State.

The pergola of stone columns roofed by vines runs
alongside a topiary parterre composed of very low
box-hedges on a terrace of stone chippings.

The rooms run one into the other down both wings and across the two cross-wings which link them. Passages have been made by the present owner's grandfather to give more privacy to the bed-rooms, but the main rooms are still *en suite,* and one can imagine them as the scene of neighbourly reunions, not for receptions on a princely scale. They are simple and sturdy. They have two remarkable features, their ceilings and their doors. The carpentry of the house is excellent, executed in Spanish chestnut, which has been enriched as well as preserved by frequent oiling. The ceilings are coved and strongly ribbed, leaving triangular spaces between the ribs and room for carved cartouches in the centres. Much ingenuity is displayed in varying the shapes of these ceilings, for though the rooms are always rectangular, we have octagonal, hexagonal, square and vaulted ceilings, all executed in the same heavy, shining wood. The internal doors have pediments above them carved with great delicacy and invention. Here the baroque is far less voluptuous than outside the house. The wood is dark and it is not too easy to distinguish in the shadows the *putti* and horn-blowing angels which make up these elaborate mantels, but they are of far higher quality than the family portraits that adorn the walls, and once again one is surprised by the contrasts of Mateus – rough and refined, slapdash and delicate – which successive owners not only tolerated but welcomed. The cupboard doors form another illustration of this. The house is full of cupboards, several to a room, built in the thickness of the wall, and each is closed by double-leafed doors of excellent craftsmanship. How strange to lavish such care upon them and comparatively little on the furniture!

It is only in the last thirty years that the garden has been developed into the lovely classical garden which we see today. It is terraced, and the terraces lead to the vineyards without any noticeable break between garden and countryside, for what else is a vineyard than a garden? But close to the house we find a skilful use of hedges and retaining walls, some so small as to be mere runnels of box on a terrace of stone chips, some so large as to form a cypress tunnel so compact that the individual trees are lost in the rotundity of the whole. The garden is the latest addition to Mateus, which survives not as a museum piece or a folly but a house full of animation, hospitality and fun.

Stratford Hall *Virginia USA 1725-30*

Stratford has belonged since 1929 to the Robert E. Lee Memorial Foundation, and they have done the nation a service in rescuing from dereliction a house of quite exceptional interest. By the terms of its charter the Foundation hold Stratford 'in perpetual memory of Robert E. Lee', the Confederate general. This has had the effect of focussing attention upon a single figure and one comparatively small incident in its long and distinguished history. It is true that Lee was born there in 1807, but his family moved to Alexandria near Washington when he was only three and, apart from childhood visits, he never went there again. So seekers after memorials of this great man are often surprised to discover, instead of the shuttered mansion with tall slim columns which they expected, an austere, almost un-American, house which many of them find, at first glance, gaunt. The only trace of the General is the bedroom where he was born.

The open secret of the place is that it was built eighty years before that auspicious birthday, and that it has produced more patriots who have left their mark on American history than any other house in the country. Thomas Lee, its builder, was Acting-Governor of Virginia and Commander-in-Chief of the colony's armed forces in 1749, and by his diplomacy opened up the whole Ohio basin to British colonial settlement. Two of his sons, Richard Henry and Francis Lightfoot, were among the signatories of the Declaration of Independence, and Robert E. Lee's father, 'Light-Horse' Harry Lee, was Washington's favourite cavalry commander. It is not surprising that when Robert E. Lee's fighting days were over, he should have wanted to buy back the family house from the strangers into whose hands it had passed. But he had neither the money nor the opportunity, for Stratford was not then for sale.

The house which nurtured so phenomenal a family was itself a phenomenon. No house like it had ever been seen in America or was ever to be seen again. Erected in 1725-30, it was the first

OPPOSITE *This is the centre of the house, but it is not its main entrance, which was at the side. At once one notices the architectural originality of Stratford – chimneys linked to form a belvedere, and an extraordinary staircase of corbelled stone, narrowing as it mounts to the main saloon.* ABOVE *Thomas Lee (1690-1750), the builder of Stratford, a portrait by an unknown artist of the British school. He spent several months of the year 1716 in England, and began the building of his new house in about 1725, clearly influenced by what he had seen abroad.*

mansion in Virginia to be constructed entirely of brick. It was the first to be built on the Tudor H-plan, with the hall occupying the bar, and the wings the uprights, of the H. It was the first to place its main reception rooms on the first floor and the bedrooms on the ground floor. Its chimneys and exterior staircases remain unique in American architecture. Its hall was in shape, size and decoration far in advance of its times. Finally, but without exhausting the possible catalogue of innovations, its garden was the finest private garden in the colonies, forming a bond between the house and the 16,000-acre plantation which encircled it.

The site is about a mile from the vast estuary of the Potomac in the Northern Neck of Virginia, some seventy miles south-east of Washington. It is wooded country, rolling and ravined, but harnessed by well-ordered roads and paths, slab-fences, frequent lodges and agricultural buildings. The fields, scalloped out of the woods, produce corn, cane, tobacco, cattle and race-horses. There is an impression that much wood has been hewn here and much water drawn. In the middle of this gleaming estate, at the crossing-point of four avenues, Thomas Lee's house rises from fields trimmed into lawns.

To the modern taste the house appears unclothed, and almost barrack-like in its brick simplicity. No carriage-drive leads to the central steps, no plants grow at its foot nor the most tenuous creepers up its walls. Instead of fences and gate-posts there is a ha-ha separating lawn from fields (another Lee innovation), crossed by flat footbridges at either end. The brilliant sunlight does little to diversify this stern façade. But the visitor soon becomes aware that this is a house of great character, one which avoids every concession to mere prettiness. Its impressiveness is due entirely to its form, the architectural expression of the plain living and intellectual integrity of the family who built and inhabited it.

No architect's name is assigned to it, and the supposition is that its unusual plan and elevation were due to Thomas Lee himself. He is known to have visited England in 1716, a year or two before he purchased the land, and he may have seen something of Vanbrugh's and Hawksmoor's work, which would account for the obvious break with the Wren tradition, and for the linked

Stratford has an air of independence and stability, but its exterior is austere for so finely furnished a house. The walls are of brickwork in Flemish bond, with glazed headers in the lower storey. The house is built to the H-plan, the hall occupying the upper part of the bar, and in each of the four wings there are two rooms to a floor, a larger and a smaller. On this south side there is only a lawn. The garden, which is one of the finest in America, extends round the other three sides. The east side, in autumn, is seen on the facing page.

The great Hall at Stratford was the largest panelled room in Virginia, with a range of Corinthian pilasters unique in the colonies. It has two exterior doors, usually left open in summer for coolness. The inner door on the right leads to a corridor separating the parlour from the library.

chimneys and terraced steps. But nothing in England or elsewhere resembles the most striking feature of the front, the central outside staircase. It is a straight flight narrowing as it mounts, and flanked by heavy stone balustrades. These steps are modern reconstructions based on fragments of the original found buried in the grounds, and it seems doubtful whether they could have been built just like this. The men who displayed so excellent a sense of proportion in the rest of this building would have been unlikely to overlook the incongruity of such an approach to it. It gives the house a maladroit appearance, like a shirt-tail hanging out from a well-tailored suit.

The four exterior stairways lead directly to the main floor, raised by its 'basement' ten feet above the bedrooms at ground-level. This arrangement had become quite common in western Europe. It lent importance to the *piano nobile*, and the views from it were all the grander for being elevated. But in Virginia it had the additional advantage of cooling the reception rooms in summer and warming the bedrooms in winter. A through-draught is created by the four opposite doors of the hall, two north and south, two east and west, and one can imagine them usually left open. The hall is the centrepiece of the house both physically and socially. Although early in date, it remains the largest panelled room in colonial Virginia. Its pairs of fluted pilasters standing on each side of the four windows and eight doors (four of which are cupboards) are topped by Corinthian capitals of a rustic design which give the room a more homespun appearance than the rest of the house. It could not be called beautiful. Rather it is bold and strong and experimental. It lacks something, a fireplace perhaps, that would give it a focal point. Far more pleasing, though more conventional, are the library, the dining room, and 'Mother's Room', where all those distinguished infants were born.

216

RIGHT *The dining-room is in two parts, with an open arch between them. The house is furnished mainly with American pieces, but also with much 18th-century English furniture, because the Lees, in common with other Virginian families who prospered on trade with England, would probably have imported their finer pieces from the mother-country. 'Mother's Room' (ABOVE) in the south-east corner of the house, was where General Robert E. Lee and other earlier Lees were born. The room is furnished as it might have been at the General's birth in 1807.*

The smaller rooms at Stratford are furnished with an elegant simplicity that suggests the character of the family, and the whole house is maintained in perfect condition. OPPOSITE *This fine example of a southern colonial kitchen lies outside the main house, in one of the four dependencies. The fireplace is twelve feet wide. The furniture and utensils are of the period of Stratford's prime, many of them found on the place when it was acquired by the Robert E. Lee Memorial Foundation in 1929.*

Downstairs, on the ground level, are the bedrooms, approached either from outside or by a single twisting staircase which the women of the house must have found almost impossible to negotiate in full skirts. There are four bedrooms in each wing, eight in all, with a servants' room and storage space under the hall. These little rooms, some of which were later converted to other uses such as schoolroom and spinning room, are quite charming. They look directly on the gardens or forecourt, with plain white walls and ceilings and each a fireplace, and have been excellently furnished by the Foundation with colonial and English furniture rich in polished brass and mahogany. The simplicity and comfort of these rooms are in strange contrast to the austerity of the outside, as was obviously intended. Stratford does not overawe, but it holds its domesticity in reserve.

The mansion was the headquarters of a vast plantation. Nearest to the house, but too small and diverse and rather too distant for them to be architecturally related to it, are four 'dependencies', little brick houses, some of a single room, others of three, containing the kitchen, estate office, dairy and stores. Beyond are the smoke-house, the wash-house, stables, coach-house, a pretty octagonal pavilion (conceivably the privy, as at Mount Vernon), and among the far trees quarters for the slaves. Each of these buildings is of much interest, illustrating the village-like conception of a great house in colonial days. The reconstruction of the garden by the Gardening Club of Virginia to its approximate appearance in the time of Thomas Lee is most successful. Indeed, the best view of the house is from this east side, where the beeches, planted by Thomas as saplings, now almost touch the brickwork, and break up its angularities by leaf and shadow. One must, however, be careful not to sentimentalise this view, since the Lee family would have been the last to confuse elegance with charm.

Villa Pisani *Strà Italy 1730-40*

Frigimelica's graceful portals (of which one is seen in more detail OPPOSITE) *stand each side of the vast villa designed by his successor Francesco Preti for the Doge of Venice. The Brenta Canal is in the foreground, and between it and the house is the public road, marked by the line of stone bollards.*

There are many Villas Pisani scattered around the Veneto, for the family of Pisani was the wealthiest in Venice and widely bifurcated, but this is the largest of all their houses, more a palace than a villa, and the most imposing house on the whole length of the aristocratic Brenta canal. Its building was commissioned soon after 1730 by Alvise Pisani, Doge of Venice. His first architect was Girolamo Frigimelica, who died in 1732, and his baroque plans for the main house were then superseded by those of Francesco Maria Preti, who substituted the neo-classic style which we see today. Frigimelica's designs, however, were used for the stables, the lovely portals on each side of the entrance, and several garden pavilions. These annexes are not unimportant. They invest a monumental pile with an exhilarating elegance. They extend its compass to embrace architecturally a wide area of parkland behind, and they are in themselves graceful variants on early 18th-century themes. Frigimelica and Preti are therefore rightly commemorated as the joint architects of the Villa Pisani on a tablet set in its entrance porch.

There is no barrier between the road and the house other than a line of low stone posts with chains looped between them. The façade is open to the highway like most other villas on the Brenta. Its privacy is safeguarded by its very magnificence. Only the greatly daring or the basely impertinent would knock uninvited at so imposing an entrance. The front is formal but not austere. It has no great originality, but its stock-in-trade elements are well balanced – a frontispiece of eight Corinthian columns sunk to half their depth in the wall, below a great central pediment, and Ionic pilasters reaching out in couples to pedimented wings. Along the roofline stand urns and statues. One has seen the same

The inner entrance of the Villa Pisani was designed with much architectural ingenuity. The great rows of columns support the ballroom wing, and to the right and left extend colonnaded courts at the heart of the house. Beyond, through the open doors, is the first glimpse of the stables reflected in the long fishpond.

thing many times before, and although it is impressive, one demands, and is given, something more. Frigimelica's portals stand each side of the house, built in white stone that contrasts with the huge extent of yellow stucco between them. They have a daring, fanciful quality which the exterior of the main house lacks. It was a happy decision to incorporate them in the changed design.

Once within the front doors, we discover that Preti, too, was not content with the platitudes of Palladianism. The centre of the house is very cleverly modelled. It is formed around two colonnaded courtyards separated by a transverse wing which contains the ballroom on the upper floor, and, below, symmetrical rows of pillars and arches which support the ballroom and lead the eye through to the garden. The entrance, which in many Palladian houses was a mere pause for ascent to the *piano nobile,* here comes as a surprise and a delight. The procession of butter-yellow columns, reminiscent in their grave massing of a temple at Luxor, opens at the far end to as superb a vista as can be found on any Italian estate. A quarter of a mile away, at the base of a long ornamental lake, stand Frigimelica's stables. Alternatively, the visitor can delay his exploration of the garden, and walk round the two cloisters of the courts. Seldom can a house have afforded so much variety in so little space before even a single room has been entered.

There is no garden in the sense of flower-beds or *parterres*. It is an ornamental park. It is composed of the long canal flanked by statues on its stone rim, the stable-block at the far end, and woods of splendid trees forming the outer edges of the vista. They conceal behind their leafy frothiness several architectural frolics like a belvedere, an exedra, a maze with a tower in the middle, and subsidiary gates terminating short avenues cut through the woods. All of these lighthearted buildings repeat the confectionary qualities of Frigimelica's entrance portals. The most enticing of all, for it draws every visitor towards it, is his stable building. It has the apparent size and elevations of a considerable villa. In fact, there was only room in it for two dozen horses. That such care and expense should have been expended for so modest a purpose may seem surprising, but the stables had another and more important function. They provided a terminal point for the view from the house (a necessity which no Italian garden of any size could be without), and a method of concealing the fact that the property is rounded off at this point by a public road. The extreme thinness of the building is not realised until you peer through its gates and see the road immediately outside. It is a piece of scenic *trompe l'œil*. Who could believe that so important and central a building was little more than a lodge, and that it stood at the very confines of the estate?

The view of Frigimelica's stable-block from the garden-front of the house. It looks like another considerable villa, but there are no rooms there, only stalls for a score of horses. It was given this grandiose façade in order to provide a terminal point for the all-important vista from the house. The fishpond was added in the late 18th century following Frigimelica's intention.

Returning to the main house, we mount a pompous staircase to the *piano nobile*. At first it seems disappointing. Room leads into room through rather cheap modern doors, and in none of them is there much furniture or painting worth a second glance. The rooms are left authentically bare, because the 18th century preferred them that way, and they have the slight melancholy of all palaces where tourists and schoolchildren have taken the place of courtiers. Two of the rooms are of special historical interest: the room and the bed where Napoleon slept after making the Villa Pisani his own in 1807; and the room at the opposite end of the house where Mussolini and Hitler first conferred in June 1934. But nothing hitherto seen prepares us for the most ravishing surprise of the villa, its ballroom.

It is one of the most splendid 18th-century rooms to have survived intact. Even if Tiepolo had never painted its ceiling, it would still be a room worth crossing continents to visit. It is very large and very high. It is surrounded on all sides by a suspended gallery of gilded wood, and painted with architectural motifs framing pale yellow panels between the windows. The two doorways are tall narrow arches fitted to half their height with bronze gates. The predominant colours are ivory and gilt and the porphyry of the floor, to which are added dashes of blue and red in Tiepolo's 'Apotheosis of the House of Pisani' which extends

ABOVE *This bedroom was furnished for Napoleon, who occasionally stayed at the Villa Pisani. It was subsequently used as his headquarters by Eugène de Beauharnais, who ruled Italy as Napoleon's viceroy.*
RIGHT *The ballroom, of which the ceiling was painted by Gian Battista Tiepolo in 1761-2. It is a magnificent illustration of the luxury of the country-houses built by the Venetian nobility.*

TOP RIGHT *A suspended gallery with a richly ornamented balustrade runs round the ballroom at the Villa Pisani. Some of the architecture above it is real ; some of it is painted in* trompe l'oeil. *Note the dangling hoof in the top corner, a typical conceit of Mengazzi-Colonna, Tiepolo's collaborator.* ABOVE *One of the four chandeliers in the ballroom, worked in wood and metal by P. Visconti.* OPPOSITE *A detail of the ballroom ceiling, with a corner of Tiepolo's great painting,* 'The Apotheosis of the House of Pisani.'

across the whole cartouche formed by the ceiling. It was the last work he executed before leaving Italy for Spain in 1762. His favourite collaborator, Mengazzi-Colonna, painted the exquisite architectural detail on the walls and those dizzy perspectives of which he was master, so ingenious that all that can be seen of one convincing figure at the ceiling's edge are the soles of his shoes. Splendid chandeliers of wood and metal by P. Visconti hang like spiders in the four angles of the room. It is an amazing achievement of architecture, *trompe l'œil*, straight painting, metalwork and carving. Its richness is muted by its great size, but no assembly would have found it unworthy of the finest occasions. Here the Doge received his guests and Napoleon his adulators ; from here Eugène de Beauharnais ruled Italy as Napoleon's Viceroy ; here the King entertained, and here Mussolini. Since 1882 it had been the property of the State.

In any other European country the date 1730-40 would arouse expectations of art and architecture as fine as that country ever produced ; in Italy it arouses apprehension that the best is past. The Villa Pisani is a reminder that the 18th century in Italy could still set standards of new perfection. If its exterior is slightly unpromising and its living rooms gloomy, its courtyards, park and ballroom can be counted among the nation's finest accomplishments.

Schloss Fasanerie *Fulda Germany 1737-56, 1820-6*

The estate lies in the deep countryside of central Germany, a few miles from Fulda. The airview ABOVE *shows the four courtyards, of which the upper two are agricultural. The original house of the Bishops of Fulda is the smaller of the two cross-wings, and in 1737-56 they added the two side wings and the main cross-wing with the high roof. The latter, seen in more detail* OPPOSITE, *was rebuilt in 1820-21 by the Elector William II of Hesse, and contains on its floor the great hall of the Electors.*

Red roofs and two helmeted towers rise above a sea of dark trees. It is a very large house set in an 'English' park, but it is only from the air that its true size is apparent. Then it can be seen that the house consists of four great courtyards, one opening from behind another, and that it is the centre of an agricultural estate as well as the seat of a great family. To walk from one courtyard to the next is to move from high civilization to its source – the land. Horses still clatter over the cobbles of the innermost court, and honest farmyard smells tease the nose. Indeed, the agricultural connections of the Fasanerie (the 'pheasant hatchery') have affected its entire character. It was built for the Bishops of Fulda between 1737 and 1756 by Andreas Gallasini, but its exterior is neither Italian, nor episcopal, nor particularly baroque. It is a strong, bold, bucolic manor-house of great size, its mansard roofs and twin towers forming almost its only external decoration. It is country architecture, unsophisticated and solid. Today it appears from outside not to be in very good condition, for plaster is seen to be flaking from some of the walls. Nothing could be more deceptive. The Fasanerie contains a large suite of rooms which are staggering for their beauty and perfect state, and these rooms contain works-of-art any one of which could be the most treasured possession of a family of more modest means. The surprise of finding such an interior within such an exterior is part of the pleasure which it gives. It is like picking up a diamond in a farmyard.

The bishops did not inhabit their summer-palace for long. In 1815 it was made over to the Landgraves of Hesse-Kassel, to whom it still belongs, and between 1820 and 1827 the long southern wings and the central blocks were rebuilt by the Elector William II, who employed an architect from Kassel, Johan Conrad Bromeis. Thus, ignoring minor complications, we must distinguish two main periods in the house; first, the exquisite baroque of the Bishops of Fulda, including the great staircase and the rooms on the first floor of the north wing. Secondly, the remainder of the State rooms in the south wing and cross-wing which constitute a German palace of the immediate post-Napoleonic age.

Both are masterpieces of their style, but neither would have survived the political and military ravages of the 20th century had it not been for the present Prince Philip of Hesse, who has remade these rooms and furnished them with some of the treasures of his family's art-collection, to which he has added much of his own acquisition. Indeed his work of restoration and display deserves to stand equal with the work of construction and decoration undertaken by the bishops and the Landgraves in the past. It was not simply a question of patching stucco and mending furniture. It was a re-creation of two ages, spread roughly from the mid-18th-century to the mid-19th, with overlaps at each end; and assembling within a great house a collection of all forms of decorative art from many countries and periods in order to create a museum-within-a-house. Part of the Fasanerie is openly a museum. There are glass show-cases on the ground floor containing porcelain and silver which clearly will never be removed from them, and should not be, for they are far too valuable to use. On the same floor, and again in one of the State rooms above, are displayed a quantity and variety of Greek, Roman and Egyptian antiquities which could never have been distributed through the living-rooms even of a palace without overburdening them. In 1967 two more rooms had to be added to contain them. The other rooms in the house, however, have been refurnished as habitable rooms, and are occasionally inhabited. Among these are the very grand reception rooms of the early 19th-century Landgraves, and a series of small suites, some dating from the occupation of the house by the Bishops of Fulda, and some more recent.

There are two aspects of these rooms which should be noted. The first is a purely practical one: the house is superbly shown. This in itself is a minor art, rendered all the more difficult in this case by the value of the collection on display. It would be impossible to allow members of the public to wander through the house unaccompanied, and guided tours are arranged at stated intervals. This means that guard-ropes, prohibitory notices and other ugly impediments can to a great extent be eliminated; and the use of felt over-shoes on parquet floors renders unnecessary the drugget strips which can destroy a room's appearance. Secondly, the collection is not all indigenous to the house. Most of it has been assembled here since 1945 by Prince Philip of Hesse from other family properties such as Wilhelmshöhe near Kassel, Rumpenheim near Offenback, a third Hesse *château* near Frankfurt and a fourth on the Danish frontier. He had remodelled

ABOVE *The baroque staircase-hall at the Fasanerie survives from the second period of the Bishops of Fulda, 1737-56, and is one of the finest in Germany. It is known as the Emperors' Staircase from the twelve busts of Caesars in the window-niches. The busts are of stucco imitating marble, like the large white vases standing on the balustrade. They are matched below by 18th-century paintings of the emperors of the Holy Roman Empire.* OPPOSITE *One of the Tischbein paintings in the Heron Hall at the Fasanerie, showing the château of Wabern, for which the pictures were originally made.* BELOW *Among the most important treasures of the house are collections of silver, porcelain and antique sculpture. This splendid travelling-case is one of the loveliest objects on display.*

entire rooms at the Fasanerie in order to contain works of art from these other houses : for instance, the *Reiher-Saal* contains the six lovely paintings of falconry by Tischbein the elder, made in 1756 for a hunting-lodge at Wabern, near Fritzlar ; and his newly finished gallery of antique sculpture is lined with paintings of other Hesse properties removed hither from Rumpenheim. Thus one problem of great proprietors has been brilliantly solved. What can one do with priceless family heirlooms when the houses which contained them have been destroyed or are too large to maintain ? The usual answer is to sell them or bank them : here a third, and better, answer has been found : amalgamate them. Bring together the best of a family's collection in one house, and by judicious arrangement, sometimes by period, sometimes according to scale and colour, contrive new rooms which will be both lovely to look at and a historical reminder.

The two branches of the family, Hesse-Kassel and Hesse-Darmstadt, were widely connected with other ruling houses of Europe, particularly the English, the Russian and the Scandinavian. The Fasanerie is full of reminders of these links, in the form of

OPPOSITE *The Heron Hall is called after the six large canvasses of heron-hawking by Johann Heinrich Tischbein the Elder, painted in 1756 for the Hesse hunting-lodge of Wabern near Fritzlar. They were reassembled in this room at the Fasanerie by Prince Philip of Hesse.* BELOW *The collections at the Fasanerie are arranged in a manner which perfectly combines the characters of a museum and a house. This is one of the most recently formed rooms, hung with portraits of the Governors of Maastricht.*

family portraits or pieces of furniture included in a bride's dowry. One advantage of a ruling family is that its pedigree is not likely to be lost, and members of it to the ninth and tenth generations and beyond remain identifiable personalities with identifiable possessions. Another is that the international ramifications at this level of society are so extensive that a house will rapidly fill with works-of-art from many countries, always among the choicest products of each successive age. Thus a visitor set down unexpectedly in the Fasanerie would not easily discover that he was in Germany, unless the staircase, with its wonderful baroque ceiling, gave the secret away. He might in one corner think himself at Malmaison; in another, at Windsor; in a third, at the Villa Pisani, illustrated elsewhere in this volume; or in Vienna. Apart from the Biedermeier furniture and decoration, derived from the French Empire style, there is little in the post-1820 part of the house which stamps it as distinctively German, although it was created by a great German family in a great German house. One's impression is of high international taste maintained over several generations; and of the outstanding quality of the European decorative arts continuing well into the middle of the 19th century. Anyone who believes that good design ended with Napoleon should spend two or three hours in this house.

ABOVE *The Empire cradle in the 'Danish bedroom' at the Fasanerie has held all the Hessian princes since it was made for Schloss Rumpenheim in the early 19th century.* TOP LEFT *'Anyone who believes that good design ended with Napoleon should spend two or three hours in this house.' The Garden Room is papered with brilliant scenes from Greek mythology, made by the French artist Dufour in 1825-27. Beside the piano is a marble bust of Frederick-William II, King of Prussia, by Gottfried Schadow.* OPPOSITE *The dressing-room of Alexandra Nikolajewna, daughter of Czar Nicholas I, who married the Landgrave Frederick-William of Hesse in 1843. She died in the next year, aged 19. The table-mirror and silver candlesticks came with her dowry from St Petersburg. The chandelier and wall-mirror are of contemporary Meissen porcelain.*

But in the end, after all the chaste gold and silver, brocade and silks, of the Hessian Electors, it is to the Bishops of Fulda that one returns. The most beautiful part of the house is the baroque. The rooms are smaller and warmer. Tendrils of gilded stucco lick the ceilings like little flames, and the walls are clothed in tapestry – in one small cabinet with *chinoiserie* – which renders intimate what is undeniably grand. The rooms open up one after the other from a long corridor which passes the head of the staircase at its mid-point. We look into 'the English rooms' and 'the Danish rooms', and finally arrive at a sitting-room furnished exactly as it might have been, and perhaps was, in about 1850. In this most modest of more than forty rooms shown to the public we seem to have arrived at a consummation of everything seen hitherto – a room in which nothing is ugly, and everything is individual to its age and original owners, a habitable (and, in fact, frequently in-habited) room, warm and much treasured, the room of a family who have cared for things and people. How strange to find the essence of this magnificent house in a mid-Victorian boudoir! But it is so. And to have preserved it just like this, when another might have pitched 'this rubbish' away, is typical of Prince Philip's sense of period and design with which he has enhanced everything he has touched.

ABOVE *This room, as the ceiling indicates, is in the baroque part of the Fasanerie, but the walls are covered in French calico, hand-printed in 1790. The portraits are of members of the families of the Electors and Landgraves of Hesse. Beyond, in the adjoining room, is a travelling bed.* RIGHT *The Blue Bedroom is also in the baroque wing. The walls are covered in blue damask of 1765. The furniture, including the bed crowned with ostrich feathers, dates from the last third of the 18th century.* OPPOSITE *The mid-Victorian boudoir, furnished in the style of about 1850, is 'warm and much treasured, the room of a family who have cared for things and people.'*

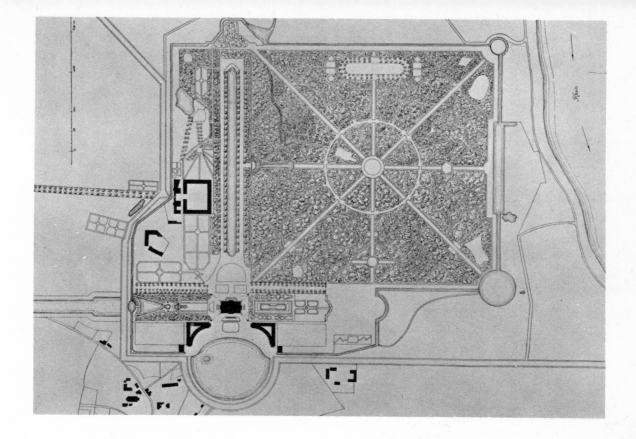

Schloss Benrath *Düsseldorf Germany 1755-73*

A pink pavilion reflected in a lake is the first sight which the visitor obtains of this wonderful building before he is clear of the suburban trams of Düsseldorf. It is a pity that its entrance should be so cluttered, but the City of Düsseldorf, which has owned the house since 1929, has done its utmost. At least the lake remains to divide house from town, and the curving outbuildings, once reserved for courtiers and kitchens, still hold the world at arm's length. On the park-side its serenity is undisturbed except by the distant hum of urgent machinery, and an alternative approach, well worth the effort, is the 15-minute walk from the Rhine through the magnificent woods. A corner of the house, a slice of cake coated in pink icing, is visible from the far end of the great avenue. Suddenly the black tree-trunks halt with uniform precision, and you are on the terrace, sharing it with six statues poised to sprint the length of the canal which faces them. The house is at their backs.

Its smallness and simplicity are both deceptive. This apparent one-storey pavilion has in fact four – three above ground and one below – and it contains in all 86 rooms, some of them of a very considerable size. There is a pronounced swagger in the flow of

ABOVE *A plan of the house and its park at the end of the 18th century. It is little different today. The house itself is shown in solid black in the bottom-left quarter of the plan. Below it are the two bracket-wings for the servants and courtiers, and below them, the nut-shaped lake. The park is set at 45 degrees from the house, its radiating avenues leading to the Rhine, the banks of which are indicated on the extreme right.*
OPPOSITE *Part of the west side of the house from the English garden, which is matched at the opposite end by a more formal French garden. From this aspect Benrath appears a one-storey building, but it has four.*

239

LEFT *A cross-section through the length of the house, from the original drawing by the architect of Benrath, Nicolas de Pigage. In the centre is the domed hall or Kuppelsaal, and on either side extend the main reception-rooms of the Elector and Electress. The basement was for storage and servants' access. There were no kitchens in the main block.* BELOW *The entrance front, with its two detached wings, seen from across the lake. The main road to Düsseldorf runs along the near bank, and this is the view that bursts suddenly upon the motorist before he is clear of the industrial suburbs. The City has owned Benrath since 1929.*

the exterior, and a good-humoured audacity about it which makes an Englishman regret the cold classicism of the Palladian style, contemporary in his own country with this more exciting rococo abroad. Look at the windows – those below are as high as doors, each fitted with a canopy, while those at roof-level are *œils-de-bœuf* transformed by twirling stone into oval frames worthy of portraits or mirrors. Look at the roof itself, a covering solid enough, but no part of it is at rest ; it fits the house like a sinuous dragon's skin, and the tiles flip over each other like scales. On the top is a lantern recalling a classical pediment only in its triangularity, for it is untrammelled by cornices, and exhibits to us Diana surrounded by symbols of the chase, a stag, a net and some hounds. A boy with a hunting horn has seemingly strayed towards them along the eaves.

The whole house is rounded, cushioned and tasselled ; a pavilion, a lodge, apparently dedicated to pleasure and country pursuits. But it is equally evident that it was the house of someone very grand, for such simplicity is not attained except at great cost. One's mind flashes to Sans Souci or the Amalienburg, also low pavilions with swelling centres. Benrath was indeed almost a royal palace. It was commissioned in 1755 by the Elector, Karl Theodor, the ruler since 1742 of the Duchy of Berg, and his architect was a Frenchman, Nicolas de Pigage. It was a very long time before it was finished. The Seven Years War interrupted the work soon after it was begun, and then the sheer complexity of the decorations and internal arrangements made progress slow. It was not until 1773 that the main house was complete ; the wings took a few years longer. But in 1778 the Elector, whose main residence was in any case at Mannheim, became Elector of Bavaria and was required to move to Munich. Benrath was therefore inhabited by its owner for far less time than it had taken to build it. After his death in 1799, it remained tenantless. Napoleon's marshal, Joachim Murat, held his court there for two years, and in the 19th century members of the Prussian royal family

TOP *The sculptural centrepiece of the garden-front stamps it with the character of a hunting lodge. Diana, holding a net, is flanked by hounds and a stag.* ABOVE *A horn-blowing putto mounted on the cornice of the garden front. To the right is one of the oeils-de-boeuf 'transformed by twirling stone into oval frames worthy of portraits or mirrors.'*

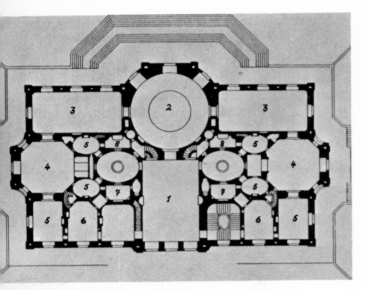

TOP *A portrait of Nicolas de Pigage, the architect of Benrath, painted by Anna Dorothea Lisiewska in 1764. He was born in Lunéville in 1723, and studied in Paris, Italy and England before entering the service of Karl Theodore. Benrath is undoubtedly his masterpiece, and he worked on it from 1755 to 1780.* ABOVE *The ground-plan of the house shows the extraordinary ingenuity of its construction. The entrance-hall (1) leads to the circular Kuppelsaal (2), from which the two main reception-rooms branch right and left (3). The bedrooms of the Elector and Electress are at opposite ends (4) and were connected to tiny cabinets (5) lit by oval light-wells with circular fountains in the middle.* OPPOSITE *One of the stucco reliefs of the four Elements in the hall. This one, with the salamander, represents fire.*

would spend there an occasional summer holiday. Otherwise it has known only tourists and the guests of the municipality or organisations who borrow the house for evening receptions.

But it remains a house. It has bedrooms, bathrooms, closets for hanging clothes, and passages and private staircases to ensure privacy of approach. Upstairs there are suites of rooms – each consisting of a bedroom, a sitting-room and a 'cabinet' for undressing – which are finished to the same point of perfection as the rooms below. Tucked under the roof is a further set of rooms for servants. All these are arranged with a clockmaker's ingenuity within a very confined space, so that if one could take Benrath to pieces like a doll's house, it would require a careful plan or an exceptional memory to put it together again. Yet inside there is never any feeling of constriction. No door is too low to pass through without stooping, and no room too small for its purpose. That is the point : the scale of every room has been matched to the scale of the activity for which it was designed. You do not need a room in which to prepare for bed, for dinner or for a bath : you need a 'cabinet' with well-fitted cupboards all around. Similarly, it is a waste of space to use the room where you sleep only for sleeping : close off your bed-alcove by doors in the day-time and you have an extra private sitting-room. It is the same with the shapes of rooms as with their size : the conventional rectangle is excellent for a large reception room, but an octagon makes an interesting shape for the placing of windows, furniture and mirrors ; while ovals, particularly small ovals, give an extra sense of privacy and enclosure (the egg and the womb ?), and are used here profusely for the small rooms in the house, including the bathrooms, and for the tiny internal courtyards.

Nicolas de Pigage must have spent many hours at his drawing-board working out the puzzle of Benrath's various floor-plans. There is a portrait of him in the house apparently engaged on precisely this occupation, and he is looking up, the pencil still in his hand, with an expression of alert amusement, as if he were saying to his patron or one of his many collaborators, 'Let's try it like this'. In one respect he was fortunate : Karl Theodor and his wife, Elisabeth Amalie, were barely on speaking-terms and only assumed conjugal attitudes for the sake of appearances in public. So their new Schloss was arranged with complete symmetry, providing a suite for the Elector and a separate suite for his wife. Their bedrooms were as far apart as it was possible to place them. An architectural problem solved on one side of the house was thereby also solved for the other. It would be possible to produce the whole plan of Benrath by drawing half only, and then doubling the paper over while the ink was still wet to duplicate it for the other half. Only the main staircase, which is modest, upsets the mirror-likeness of the two sets of rooms.

Two of these are central and shared – the entrance hall and the circular domed room (the *Kuppelsaal*), beyond. From the *Kuppelsaal* extend two reception-galleries, right and left, one for the Elector and one for the Electress, as their monograms above the opposite doors proclaim. In these four rooms we have a perfect example of Pigage's sense of scale. All four are large, so large that

even after studying the plans it remains astonishing that eighty further rooms can be stowed away in what is left of the house; and all have different shapes and, by analogy, different temperatures. First comes the hall or vestibule, entered by tall door-windows from outside, paved in alternate squares of black and ruddy-white marble which shine like ice. The atmosphere is cool, Italian; the colours grey and cream. On the wall-panels are stuccos of the Four Elements, varying in depth of relief from a boy's head in the round to a wisp of escaping smoke. There is almost no furniture: none is needed. But in alcoves in the centre of the side-walls stand statues of Flora and Hercules by W. Christian Meyer, works of very great beauty enhanced by the gossamer shadows of the apses enfolding them. The room was finished about 1770. Already one can see the restraint of Benrath's rococo. The prettiness of a house like Sans Souci, ten years earlier, has given way to a graver classicism, but the delicacy is still there: the delicacy and the invention.

Both are seen to even greater effect in the *Kuppelsaal*. Here again the floor is of marble, composed of pieces arranged concentrically around a central star, each piece cut precisely to a trapezoid shape which increases in size as the circles spread outwards – yet another example of the superb craftsmanship evident in every part of the house. The walls are of greyish stucco and imitation marble, divided into bays by Corinthian pilasters, two bays containing fireplaces, three with doors and three with windows. The decoration of all these elements is very rich indeed, but there is no overburden, owing to the monochrome of the stucco, the absence of gilt and the harmony of the sculpture and relief. *Putti* gambol and cuddle everywhere – around the walls, along the cornice, high up in the dome. There are enough of them in this house to fill a medium-sized nursery school. The most dizzily perched are those trailing a leg from the cupola, and the stuccoist has been persuaded to give them a pair of wings for safety's sake. High in the centre of the main dome, starred with rosettes, comes a circular opening through which we see Diana and her train painted on the outer dome. This too is pierced centrally, but irregularly, by another orifice hung with nets, and through this we see Flora on the ceiling of the lantern. The triple dome is the most ambitious conceit of Benrath. It is not its most successful. The house is too beautiful for jokes of this kind, and the paintings on the ceiling are not in perfect condition, unlike the remaining decorations of the house; such devices must be without blemish to be truly effective. It was from the gallery concealed in the cupola that musicians played and choirs sang, their music floating down as if from the very heavens. Perhaps the guests, looking upward, caught sight of an occasional wig or fluttered handkerchief in the flower-goddess's preserve; but the best view was that obtained by the musicians themselves, who would have watched the exquisite movements of a waltz against the marble patterned floor. Benrath was built for luxury; it should be used luxuriously.

The greatest glory of the other downstairs rooms, indeed of the whole house, are the parquet floors. There is no place in the world

TOP *In one wall of the hall at Benrath stands this beautiful statue of Flora, by W. Christian Meyer (1726-86).* ABOVE *The Kuppelsaal, looking into the Electress's Garden Room or reception-room. Her monogram, EA for Elisabeth Amalie, is above the door. This circular hall, completed in about 1766, rises the full height of the house. The decoration, though rich, is not over-elaborate, since the Corinthian pilasters, apparently supporting the dome, restore the necessary strength.* OPPOSITE *Looking down onto the floor of the Kuppelsaal from the outer dome.*

TOP *The octagonal bedroom of the Electress, looking through to her private sittingroom. The floor is one of the most beautiful at Benrath, with a central cartouche outlined in ebony.* ABOVE *The Elector's bathroom is an imitation in stucco of a grotto formed by oak leaves and twigs. A pair of young fawns hold an ornamental vase.* OPPOSITE *One of the smaller cabinets upstairs, which has recently been restored by woodworkers as skilled as those who laid the original parquet floors, the glory of Benrath.*

where this minor art can be seen demonstrated to greater perfection. So bewitching are the effects here obtained by the use of different coloured woods that they seem more like the products of cabinet-makers than of floor-layers. The patterns vary from room to room, no two the same, and are executed in the natural grain and colour of the woods : no staining was permitted. A particularly elegant arabesque outlined in black fills the centre of the floor in the Electress's bedroom. It seems impossible that the black can be natural. It is ; it is ebony. No wonder that visitors are required to wear felt slippers when wandering through the house ; and no wonder that Germany has been searched for woodworkers with sufficient recollected skill to repair the floors of the upper storey. Such workers were discovered, and during the past ten years a whole new range of rooms under the roof, including the chapel, have been opened to the shuffle of a delighted public.

Benrath is without question one of the great masterpieces of domestic architecture and interior decoration to have survived from the European 18th century. We still have a tendency to think of German art in terms either of spikiness and Dürer or of flamboyant baroque. Benrath is neither. It is true that Pigage was a Frenchman, but the names of the painters Lambert Krahe and F. A. Leydensdorf, the sculptor P. A. Verschaffelt, the woodcarver Augustin Egell, all of whom left works at Benrath, show that German artists too were in full command of this intoxicating style. Their patron was a German, and the site is in the heart of the Ruhr. But the spirit is European – a mixture of fancy and logic, *Dichtung und Wahrheit.* Stuccoed ribbons and flowers hang loose from the ceilings to indicate that gravity has not lost quite all its efficacy, but little *putti* squeeze uncomfortably into positions which they would abandon in thirty seconds, but are condemned to occupy for ever.

Mount Pleasant

Philadelphia USA c.1760

Set this building down in England on the outskirts of a cathedral town, and it would pass at first glance as an exceptionally fine private house of about 1730. On looking closer, there are several features which one would find puzzling. For example, that galleried bridge on top of the hipped roof, those strong chimneys with open arches on each side (is there an echo here of Vanbrugh?), the Frenchified consoles flanking the dormer-windows, and the slightly concave roofs of the two detached buildings in front. The house is American, not British, and it was built in the early 1760s. The style is Georgian, but Georgian with a built-in time-lag and a colonial distinctiveness. All the elegances of the style are there, all the proportions that had been the mark of fine architecture since Queen Anne, and a controlled display of classical elements. But how bold, how excellent, are the departures from the purely English manner! American connoisseurs have found Mount Pleasant rather ostentatious, *nouveauriche*. It does not appear so to an English eye accustomed to greater Palladian flamboyance at home. If there is a single fault in these façades (those of the entrance and garden fronts are almost identical, and those at the sides are blank), it is the slight awkwardness with which the pediment of the outside door impales with its apex the Venetian window above. But the design of the door and window is as sympathetic to the English originals as the combination of brick, stone, wood and stucco across the whole width of the façade.

Mount Pleasant was called by John Adams in 1775, 'The most elegant country seat in the northern colonies'. The two flanking pavilions, forty feet from the main house, were for servants and offices. This entrance front is exactly duplicated on the other side, where a garden slopes down towards the valley.

Mount Pleasant lies a few miles from the centre of Philadelphia in Fairmount Park. It was built for John Macpherson, a Scottish mariner turned American privateer, who was a man of science and culture as well as a sea-dog, and counted among his friends John Adams, the second President of the United States, and Benedict Arnold, to whom he sold the house in 1779. Having dined with Macpherson one evening in September 1775, Adams wrote in his journal, 'He has the most elegant seat in Pennsylvania, a clever Scotch wife and two pretty daughters.' Posterity has endorsed the first of these compliments, while taking the other two on trust. Mount Pleasant is the finest surviving mansion in the central group of colonies. That the architect is unknown is strange, for the Carpenters' Company of Philadelphia was nearly forty years old when Macpherson bought the site in 1761, and its members were builder-architects who were all known by their names and works.

Captain Macpherson knew exactly what he wanted. He wanted a summer residence within easy riding-distance of central Philadelphia where he also had a town house. He wanted a place where it would be possible to entertain modestly in an imposing setting, and where two or three people (there are only two bedrooms) could spend an occasional night. The servants and kitchen were banished to the two outlying lodges, spaced forty feet on each side of the main block and quite detached from it – the only known example north of Virginia where this attractive method of freeing the house from architectural and human encumbrances was adopted.

As the Captain's needs were relatively simple, there was room within the house for him to spread himself. Mount Pleasant is light and airy. Between its five rooms (two on the ground floor, three upstairs) two hallways of generous width extend the full depth. The staircase is tucked neatly into an angle away from the hall itself. It was therefore a most welcoming place, with room to greet the guests before they entered the main saloons. But it is surprisingly small. You can see it all in ten minutes.

LEFT *Captain John Macpherson, the builder of Mount Pleasant, was a sea-commander who made a fortune by privateering. He was nine times wounded in battle with the French and Spaniards, and lost his right arm.* BELOW *The Georgian repertory is used with fascinating sureness and variety both inside and outside Mount Pleasant. The* walls are of rough-cast masonry covered with a stucco-like material and scored in imitation of ashlar, with bold quoins of red brick at the corners. The design of the Palladian window is obviously English in inspiration, but the chimneys, dormers and roof-bridge owe much to American invention.

The drawing-room, looking towards the hall and staircase. Mount Pleasant has been furnished by the Philadelphia Museum of Art with late 18th-century American pieces of the highest quality.

It is worth staying longer. There are few better examples in all America of a Georgian interior of the immediately pre-Revolution age. While other houses like the neighbouring Cliveden and Powel House were ornamented more richly, Mount Pleasant was given by its carpenters and carvers a cleanliness and crispness of detail which provokes, not astonishment, but gratification that something so difficult could be done so well. In part its decoration was taken from such bibles of the art as Abraham Swan's *British Architect*, published in 1745. But it is the combination of stock Georgian devices that is here so satisfactory. The upper drawing-room (called by Macpherson, most inappropriately, the Great Chamber) has along one wall a fireplace with an ornamental frame above it, and on each side a two-leafed arched cupboard with a broken pediment supported by carved brackets. Ask an amateur to design a wall to these specifications, and watch the

muddle that he will produce: then look at the photograph re-produced on this page, and see the reality. So low is the relief that the design is almost part of the wall, and so unemphatic is it that it comes as a surprise to discover that in the mouldings above the picture, Philadelphian carvers were already playing with the *rocaille*. In the rest of the house the detail is equally careful and re-strained. A complete Greek entablature of triglyphs and me-topes along the walls of the hall is only perceived by taking a long hard look. This was the point of Georgian detail: it was a matter of suggestion more than of assertion. It is like a fine carpet: you would feel its absence more than notice its presence.

The Captain overspent his fortune. He was obliged to put Mount Pleasant up for sale some five years after its completion, and until Benedict Arnold came forward as a purchaser, he let it to the Spanish envoy in Philadelphia. In the Revolutionary War the family was divided, one son, John, being killed fighting on the rebel side at Quebec, and the other, William, taking a commis-sion in the English army. The old Captain himself died a pauper. Arnold never occupied the house, since he fled to England to escape the consequences of his treachery to the American cause and his property was confiscated. Between 1781 and 1792 the house was bought and sold four times. Jonathan Williams, the first superintendent of West Point, purchased it in the latter year and his family held it until 1853. Shortly afterwards it became the property of the City of Philadelphia, which it remains today. The Museum of Art has furnished it with American colonial pieces of first quality, among which is a winged armchair which be-longed to Captain Macpherson himself. It is pleasant to imagine him seated before one of his great Venetian windows, contemplat-ing his garden and, beyond it, the Schuylkill River winding down to the sea.

TOP *The 'Great Chamber' on the first floor of Mount Pleasant is a superb example of elaborate wood-carv-ing. The porcelain in the cupboard is export-Chinese. Above the fireplace is a portrait by Benjamin West of Mary Keen, who married Captain Macpherson's son, William.* ABOVE *The first-floor corridor runs from front to back of the house, and the Palladian window is duplicated at the other end. Mount Pleasant is planned on a very generous scale, and its architecture is carried indoors, displaying almost every device of the classical tradition.*

253

Monticello *Virginia USA   1767-1809*

Thomas Jefferson, a portrait by Rembrandt Peale.
OPPOSITE *The garden front, which Jefferson began to rebuild in 1792 after his return from Paris. 'With extraordinary skill, he contrived to make the house seem smaller while actually doubling it in size.' The dome was the first in any American building.*

You can visualize Monticello either as Thomas Jefferson's home or as Thomas Jefferson's house. If the former, there is enough to satisfy every admirer of this most Periclean figure of America's revolutionary age, for many of Jefferson's personal belongings, and some of his furniture, have been reassembled here by the Memorial Foundation which purchased and restored the house some forty years ago. There is evidence of his taste and character in every corner of it. But it is equally rewarding to study the house as a running experiment by an amateur architect of genius : an experiment, because it incorporated so many new ideas of lasting value ; running, since Jefferson was continually remodelling it during his long life (1743-1826) ; and amateur, because he had no formal training as an architect, and a man who became in succession Governor of Virginia, American Minister in Paris, Secretary of State under Washington, Vice-President and finally President of the United States, clearly had no time for prolonged architectural study and practice. Monticello is by no means his only, or even his greatest, architectural achievement. There was the Capitol building in Richmond and his superb University of Virginia, besides various country houses which have been attributed to him with varying degrees of probability. But Monticello was his workshop in more than one sense. Here he lived and here he drew his designs ; and here he put into effect for his own pleasure his profoundest ideas of what a house should be.

As the work of an architect who also drafted the colonies' Declaration of Independence, Monticello at first sight appears unchallenging. 'In architecture he revered an authority that was not yet dead,' wrote Hugh Morrison, the American architectural historian. 'In politics he sought a freedom that was not yet born.' The authority was Palladianism. The very site and surroundings of Monticello, like its name ('little mountain'), seem Italian. Look down from the terraces and you will see deep woods leading to a plain pinpricked with white farmhouses and backed by a mountain ridge that might be part of the Apennines. In spite of all the inconvenience of a hill-top site – the labour of flattening

three acres as a platform for house and garden, the difficult ascent for carriages in country that can fill rapidly with snow – Jefferson chose it, against all precedent, because it was a hill which he had known and loved since boyhood, and because, as he wrote to a friend, 'How sublime to look down into the workhouse of nature, to see her clouds, hail, snow, rain, thunder, all fabricated at our feet!' That is one aspect of Monticello that should not be overlooked. It is romantic. But it is much else. In this single small building Jefferson expressed the contrasts of his own character – his contempt for fashion and his respect for tradition, his love of nature and his search for refinement, his desire for privacy and his sense of public responsibility. Few houses can tell one so much about the nature of the man who built it.

As completed about 1809, it was the product of two main periods of building. Starting in 1767, when he was aged 24, Jefferson planned a small cruciform house in two storeys, with an entrance front composed of two classical porticoes, two flanking wings, and a third porch on the garden side. In the course of building, every detail of which he supervised personally, he added at a lower level an octagonal bay to the end of each wing, and broke out his drawing-room into a larger octagon under the garden porch. This design was the result of toying with Palladian ideas over a number of years. One of his rough sketches for the entrance front is here reproduced, and it follows fairly closely a design for a two-storeyed portico in Leoni's edition of Palladio's *Four Books of Architecture*, a copy of which Jefferson acquired in 1769. The theme was not very satisfactory for a small house, since the superimposed porches were too heavy for the wings, and it remains in doubt whether the upper porch was ever built. But there were two features which were startlingly original and successful, and both of them survive. The first was the idea of the

ABOVE *A sketch in Jefferson's own hand, made in about 1770, for his original version of the entrance front of Monticello. It is not certain whether the Palladian idea of the two-storeyed portico was ever carried out, but if it was, it was replaced in Jefferson's lifetime by a less cumbersome porch at the same time as he added the dome.* OPPOSITE *The centre of the garden front. The drawing-room lies behind the door and two flanking windows. The snow on the steps and cupola scarcely blurs the purity of Jefferson's classical lines, and heightens the contrast in colour and texture between the stucco and the brown-ochre brick.*

octagons. They not only gave great variety to the rooms by providing wall-spaces for standing furniture at different angles and windows opening on different views, but from outside they imparted 'movement' to the whole building. Interesting effects of light and shade were thereby achieved, softening and humanising the classicism of the porches, and giving the house distinction from every angle, like a piece of sculpture. From these little octagonal rooms – a tearoom to the north, part of Jefferson's private suite to the south – you could step on to the terraces.

Here you find yourself walking on Jefferson's second brilliant innovation. He put his servants' quarters underground. They extend under and beyond the house itself, and then turn at right angles towards the garden to form two hidden wings, the stables on one side, the kitchen, dairy and smoke-room on the other, with parapet walks above them. The slope of the hill on each side is steep enough to allow an approach to these 'basements' at ground level. In this most ingenious way, made possible by the construction of his house on a flattened spine, Jefferson retained the Palladian idea of ridding his house of all the mechanisms for servicing it by putting them in adjoining wings, but cleared the decks (almost literally, for the parapet walks have the ring and freshness of a ship at sea) of all impediments to the view. He built two one-room pavilions as terminal points to the terraces, and in another structure on the site of one of them he spent his honeymoon in 1772 before the rest of the house was ready.

That was the first phase. The second (1792-1809) began some twenty years later, when Jefferson returned from his five-year residence in France as American Minister, stirred by the possibilities of the old and new European architecture that he had seen. Monticello now seemed to him clumsily provincial, and during his long absence it had fallen into a sad state of disrepair. He determined to rebuild and enlarge it, scrapping the heavy double-porch at the entrance and placing the emphasis on privacy and comfort more than on magnificence. With extraordinary skill he contrived to make it seem smaller while actually doubling it in size. The rooms facing the garden were duplicated by a parallel set of rooms on each side of a new entrance hall,

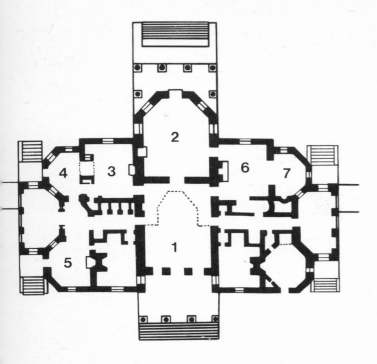

Plan of the main floor at Monticello. 1. Hall. 2. Drawing-room. 3. Jefferson's bedroom. 4. Jefferson's study. 5. Library. 6. Dining-room. 7. Tea-room. BELOW *The entrance hall, with a gallery linking the bedrooms on the floor above. Through the open doors, which are of glass, there is a glimpse of the drawing-room on the garden side.*

while the upper portico (if it was ever built) was replaced over the approximate centre of the house by a low stepped dome. 'All the good and new houses', he wrote, 'are of a single storey', and though Monticello contains four, three of them are concealed, one underground and the upper two in the roof line. A house was given the shape of a pavilion.

The immediate influence on him was without doubt French, in particular the Hôtel Beaugeon in Paris, built in 1781. But it was still essentially a Palladian idea which had been adapted to many styles, like Benrath, near Düsseldorf, or Sans Souci, Frederick the Great's rococo pleasure-palace at Potsdam, both apparent one-storey buildings with a central dome. Jefferson 'thoroughly disapproved' of contemporary English architecture, but this did not prevent him from drawing on it. The dome, which was the first to be placed over any American building, was clearly based on a plate in Robert Morris' *Select Architecture*, and on four occasions he designed a Rotunda, like Colen Campbell's and Lord Burlington's adaptations of Palladio's villa at Vicenza. For all its originality and Jefferson's admiration for the French, Monticello still looks more English than continental. This statement would not have pleased him, for he was not above allowing politics to affect his cultural judgements, but who can doubt, looking at the garden front, that the Georgian tradition is still present in the combination of russet brick and dazzlingly white woodwork, or that English Palladianism influenced the set of the house, quite apart from the romanticism of its serpentine garden-paths and the landscaping of the surrounding woods?

One weakness which it shared with contemporary English homes is that the internal convenience of the upper floors was sacrificed to external appearance. Accordingly, some bedrooms have mean little windows at floor level, and others are lit by skylights (an unsightly expedient repeated in some of the ground floor rooms, including Jefferson's own bedroom and the dining room), while the room under the dome is a fine octagon unapproachable except by tiny winding stairs and serving no apparent purpose. Jefferson called it a 'skyroom', but only a single visitor of the many who left descriptions of the house was admitted there in Jefferson's day. All the emphasis is on the suite of rooms on the ground floor, of which there are thirteen. The entrance is through the east portico into a hall with a gallery round half its upper part, and from there you look through double doors into the parlour with its five-sided bow. The use of glass in the doors is most effective, since the full depth of the house and the garden beyond are seen at once, promising comfort, hospitality and seclusion as soon as you step inside the front door. To the right is the dining room, with Wedgwood plaques let in above the fireplace (his only concession to Robert Adam), and a flattish open arch leads enticingly from it to the tearoom, an admirable example of Jefferson's flair for the intimate surprise. The decoration is French in spirit, even to the flounced curtains which he designed himself, but, as if he thought it too feminine, it is hardened by stern busts of statesmen on brackets between the windows and an imposing architrave.

Jefferson's own apartments were at the other end of the house. Here he arranged a nest of small rooms to suit a man widowed comparatively early in life. His bed, like all others in the house, was built in a recess after the French manner, but he knocked out the back panel of his own recess so that he could step out of bed on one side into his study or on the other into his dressing-room. The study adjoins his library without separating doors, and such is the irregularity of the connecting octagons and porches that the whole suite gives the impression of being much larger than it is. It is rather like a captain's quarters on a ship, but in its present restored state it is a good deal more elegant than Jefferson would have known it, for he was an untidy man, impoverished by his generosity and building extravagances, and with a passion for ethnological objects and trophies from other men's hunting expeditions which cluttered up his rooms.

If it still seems a privilege to be admitted to this corner of the house, it is a privilege enjoyed by over three hundred thousand visitors annually. The silhouette of Monticello is known to every American. It is engraved on the five-cent piece. It has come to stand, even more than Mount Vernon, for the *multum in parvo*, the decent approachability, of the Presidential line. Monticello represents a movement in architecture towards something identifiably American. Yet it was never itself imitated like Jefferson's later works. It remains the unique and very personal creation of a remarkable man, the product of observation, imagination and (as in his political and philosophical writings) a deep sense of perspective in two directions, the future and the past.

TOP *The tea-room. 'The decoration is French in spirit, even to the flounced curtains which Jefferson designed himself, but as if he thought it too feminine, it is hardened by stern busts of statesmen.'* ABOVE *Jefferson's study at Monticello, and beyond, his library. 'Such is the irregularity of the connecting octagons and porches, that the whole suite gives the impression of being much larger than it is.'*

Krengerup *Fünen Denmark c.1770*

ABOVE *A view from a first-floor window of the house across the great courtyard to the farm buildings.* OPPOSITE *The back elevation of the house is a near-duplicate of the front, but in place of the formal courtyard there is a delightful garden with an ornamental pond. The garden gradually dissolves into a small wooded park, which in turn melts imperceptibly into the surrounding farmlands.*

The date 1772 appears in the red sandstone above the entrance, and 1773 is inscribed with a flourish on a beam in the central of the many barns. Thus house and farm are contemporary and complimentary. Architecturally as well as economically they give each other support, for the farm-buildings form an open-ended square, closed, after an interval, by the house. But they do not resemble each other. The older farm buildings are half-timbered, the exposed beams painted red in the local style and the spaces between them filled with cream-coloured brick-nogging. The ridges of the thatched roofs are pegged with wooden clips. It is very feudal : the broadness of the farm-buildings suggests the broadness of the acres which they serve.

The house, in contrast, appears to owe little to the soil. It is classical, patriarchal. It disdains both sentimentality and false grandeur. There are Corinthian pilasters on the centre-piece and little iron balconies on either wing. But the owner or architect, as if contemptuous of such concessions to the outward symbols of nobility, refused to crown the house with the triangular pediment which strict classicism would have demanded, and when he came to make the steps to the front door, he omitted the balustrade. Instead, there are little lions alongside the steps and stone columns bearing lanterns. Above there are two shields leaning against each other, and an inscription. All this is relatively trivial. What makes the first impact is the bulk of the house and roof, and its colour. Its colour is white. Seldom can a mass of white have been so emphatic. It proclaims from end to end that this is a four-square, magisterial domain. There is no nonsense with curved lines or projecting wings ; no playfulness with windows of different shapes ; no irrelevant variety on the gable ends ; and when we walk round to the garden-front, here the decoration is even less – an external stairway to the central room, and that is almost all. Why then does Krengerup make an impression of such distinction ? Because of its honesty : the uncompromising horizontal lines, the sturdiness of the roof, the proportion of the windows, and the whiteness.

One is not surprised to hear that it was built by a soldier-courtier – Friderick Baron von Rantzau, who ended his career as the general commanding the Danish cavalry. His architect was Hans Naess. But when he built the house, Rantzau was young, and recently married to Baroness Sophia Magdalena Juell-Wind, so recently indeed that the initials of her maiden-name appear

OPPOSITE *The main entrance front seen across the courtyard. The architect, Hans Naess, served his apprenticeship in France and built Krengerup in the early 1770s.* ABOVE *The lock of the front door resembles a highly ornate firearm.*

alongside his own within the house. It has remained in the Rantzau family ever since, and has never been much altered. Happy the house, though unhappy the country, which has no history. There is a feeling here of undisturbed contentment symbolised by the undisturbed furniture. To explore a house where the present owner was once the infant daughter is to understand something of the accumulated affection which she has for it. The personality of Krengerup is due largely to the personalities of its past and present owners.

This is what makes the inside very different from the outside, as if the general had built the house and his wife had had her own way with the decoration and furnishing, and this had remained the division of responsibility between the sexes ever since. There is a creaminess and exuberance about the hall for which the entrance has not prepared the visitor. The stairs rise directly from inside the front door in two separated flights, joining together to mount to a first-floor landing which is supported by twin Ionic columns. The colour is basically white, but much gilded stucco strays across it. The staircase is a fine example of spatial design, creating much movement within a confined well, and from above the glimpses of the stone-flagged floor (the flags were imported from Sweden, for Denmark has no building-stone of her own) are as effective as the view of the curving balustrade from below. Clearly this will not be a dull house.

The ground-floor rooms bear out this first impression of the interior. It is large enough to contain a ballroom and both master's and mistress's bedrooms as well as a large and small sitting-room, a dining-room and a garden-room, and all these rooms flow naturally one into the other. An exit to the garden is never far away. The proportions are good, particularly of the ballroom, and the tall windows are frequent, filling the house with light. There is variety not only of scale but of colour – dark panelling in one place contrasting with yellow silk curtains and chair-covers in another, and in more than one room excellent Chinese hand-painted paper mounted on canvas, a survival, like many of the stuccoed ceilings, from the time when the house was built. There is nothing astonishing about this floor : it was not meant to astonish ; it was meant to please. It goes on pleasing two centuries later, and the reason is that nobody has since found, or probably ever will find, a better way of planning the rooms of a moderate-sized house for a family of position.

In the ballroom at Krengerup LEFT *the curtains, chairs and sofas are all of golden yellow. The Chinese wall-decorations are painted on canvas panels. On the left is one of the Norwegian stoves. Another, formed of little iron coffins separated by shining brass and dated 1741, is in the garden room* ABOVE. *The portrait is of Magdalena, Baroness Juell-Wind, painted in 1734.*

TOP *Above the door in the billiard-room at Krengerup is this delightful vignette of the game being played in the late 18th century.* OPPOSITE *In the panelled drawing-room, above an ornate door, are found these portraits by Jens Juel of the builder of Krengerup, Friderick Baron von Rantzau, and his wife, Sophia Magdalena, Baroness Juell-Wind.*

The upper floor gives equal pleasure. It consists of bedrooms and small sitting-rooms arranged on either side of a central corridor. There are nine bedrooms in all, and almost as many others which must have varied in use as the family of the day waxed and waned. One is a billiard-room today, and others were converted into bathrooms during the modernisation of the house in 1916-17. All are very simply furnished. The floors, for example, expose their unpolished planks between rugs. Many of them retain the iron Norwegian stoves from the days before central-heating was introduced, and in others there are painted vignettes from the earliest period of the house, crudely executed by local artists and craftsmen. No imported finery figures here, but the furniture is basically good, and the porcelain excellent. What pleases most is its habitableness – the natural size and disposition of the rooms, their views over farm and garden, the warm double-windows, the spaciousness of the corridors and capacity of the cupboards. Everything fits, and everything is fitting.

Around the house there is a small park which begins as a garden and ends in woodland without any firm dividing-line between them – another example of the merging of naturalness with grandeur which is the dominating characteristic of this place. Beyond the little lake the lawns splinter into the wood, creating effects of distance and a suggestion of hidden garden-temples beyond, which are not discovered by further exploration. This is the Danish countryside and Palladian conceits are not wanted here. Krengerup would make a bad museum, which is much to its credit, because it makes a delightful house.

Montgeoffroy *Maine-et-Loire France 1772-5*

The Loire is not far away from this great château, yet it is not the sort of house which immediately springs to the imagination when the *châteaux de la Loire* are mentioned. Although it has its share of bluey turrets and is built of the same milk-white stone, it is a classical, not romantic, house. It draws on the French architectural tradition and even makes use of two 16th-century towers and a little apron of a moat, survivals from the earlier château on the site, but it is conceived in a quite different spirit, an expression of the pride of the aristocracy of France in the decade before the deluge overwhelmed them. Montgeoffroy was begun in 1772 and was ready for occupation three years later.

The house was built by a soldier of great distinction, the Maréchal de Contades, who after serving Louis XV in the Corsican, Flemish and German campaigns, became Governor of Alsace and Strasbourg from 1762-88. When at the age of over seventy he came to consider his retirement, he decided to rebuild his large family house at Montgeoffroy near Angers. His architect was Nicolas Barré. At the same time he ordered in Paris all the furniture he required for his future home, submitting, one deduces from their perfect match and fit, the plans of the different rooms to the makers of the furniture, so that both were ready simultaneously. The house has not passed out of the hands of the family of de Contades since then. It was not ransacked at the time of the Revolution, owing to the respect in which the local

The present house is the third on the site. Of the first, the 16th-century house, only the moat, the angle-towers OPPOSITE *and the chapel survive. The old chapel* ABOVE *forms part of the right-hand wing and is unchanged since this drawing was made in about 1820, showing the congregation dispersing after a service. A windable watch is incorporated in the gable. The pyramid-roofed wing on the left of the drawing is the same as that shown on the right of the photograph. The full extent of the château, seen from the air, is illustrated on the next two pages.*

ABOVE *The chapel of St Catherine at Montgeoffroy, built in 1543, is one of the loveliest attached to any French private house. The building on its right was for the family's carriages, facing the stables across the entrance courtyard.* OPPOSITE *One of the turret-tops of the 16th-century towers, which also serves as a dovecot.* BELOW *The garden front of Montgeoffroy, which repeats the cool architectural lines of the main façade, and is approached by several converging avenues through thick woods.*

peasantry held the Maréchal (a story which one hears repeated so often at different châteaux in France that one begins to wonder whether the Revolution did any damage at all), and subsequent generations in the 19th century tended to leave it in the care of excellent curators. So both house and contents were saved from demolition or change. Montgeoffroy is the same house which the Maréchal knew. He could walk into it tomorrow and find his own chair, bed, gaming-board, pictures, books, precisely where he left them. The windows open in the same way on the same views. The parquet floors yield slightly to the tread of our feet as they did to his. There is plumbing and lighting which would have astonished him, but these are discreetly hidden. It is an extraordinary survival, but it is also used. Rooms which at one moment are invaded by tourists and connoisseurs become at the next the private apartments of the present Marquis de Contades. The way in which a great *seigneur* of the late 18th century chose to live is seen to be perfectly adapted to our own day. That is the surprise of Montgeoffroy. It has an air of modesty.

From outside, however, this characteristic could not be guessed. Without looking immodest, it is certainly grand. Exposed to the public view from the high-road, with three avenues converging upon it to emphasise its importance, the château lies on a gentle slope backed by a dark mass of trees which exaggerates the unusual paleness of the stone. In front we have the old round towers and the scalloped half-moat, which are linked to the main house by short service-wings containing the stables on the left and the coach-house on the right – and (an unexpected pleasure) the chapel of the old house, constructed in 1543 and dedicated to St Catherine, a strange and simple Gothic building to find alongside so much finery, and yet belonging to it. The centre is filled by the 1775 main block. Stand this building in a line with similar European buildings of the same date in an architectural identity parade, and you would immediately pick it out as French, blurred though the edges of national styles had become. It is French because of its roofs, still higher and steeper than elsewhere in Europe ; because of its *œil-de-bœuf* dormers, its shutters, and its pyramid-topped pavilions on each side. But the proportions are those which you would find in England, Italy and even Russia at this date, and the refinement of the detail (the very low relief of the De Contades arms in the pediment, for instance, and the shallow stages formed by the three groups of outside steps) is also that of an international aristocracy which had found the right note to strike, halfway between a whisper and a shout. It is not a very original exterior ; it is a culmination and anthology of other men's experiments and ideas, and as such it does not have great individuality. It is beautiful, but slightly cold. At the back, there is much more cheerfulness. Here a short avenue of plane trees, planted when the house was built, leads up to a classical 1820 temple, and a lovely wood, scarcely larger than a garden, but made to seem enormous by avenues radiating between huge trees, fills in the background to the house. The garden proper has disappeared. Old stone walls now outline its boundaries, but inside there are only vegetables and a football-pitch.

PERTE   LE ROI   GAIN

The interior of Montgeoffroy is justly celebrated in all books dealing with late 18th-century furniture and decoration. The inventory of 1775 has been preserved, noting exactly where every piece of furniture was placed at the moment when the removal vans arrived from the Paris workshops, and with this manuscript in your hands, you can wander from room to room and identify almost every piece mentioned in it. Only the curtains and carpets have disappeared, the former replaced, but the latter not, leaving the sound carpentry of the parquets exposed. On the other hand, many of the wall-coverings and bed hangings are the originals, as also are the tapestry and velvet covers to the chairs. The Maréchal de Contades made a clean sweep of his family's possessions as he did of his family's house, retaining from the 17th century only two armchairs, a clock and an Italian cabinet. The remaining pieces were made for the positions they still occupy.

These rooms are probably even more pleasant today than they were when newly furnished. The glitter of the ormolu and the colours of fresh wood, silk and wool have faded with time to produce an overall impression of muted splendour, of use and reuse. All are fitted with *boiseries,* made in Paris, and most with great wall-mirrors. They are not large rooms individually, but their double doors can be left open to form an extensive suite reaching along the whole centre of the house and from front to back. A *grand salon* occupies the place of honour in the middle, with a billiard-room (so-called in the 1775 inventory, and still containing a billiard-table) and a *petit-salon* to one side, and the Maréchal's library and bedroom on the other. Behind these are the apartments of Madame Hérault de Séchelles, the friend who brightened the last years of his life. The dining-room is said to be one of the first of its kind in France, since hitherto meals had been eaten off the moveable trestle-tables in whatever room the company happened to find itself at mealtime. Here we see a softening of the rectangular framework of the room, the nearest concession which France was making to England's cult of Adamism, for the corners are rounded and coved, and the stove-pipe is concealed by the trunk of a palm-tree in *faience.* The stove was a present to the Maréchal from Strasbourg. Another was *pâté-de-foie-gras,* invented by his chef, Klauss, and first made in a French kitchen at Montgeoffroy.

On the first floor lie the bedrooms, which open off two passages running north-south, east-west, and forming a cross in the centre of the house. These rooms too are remarkable for retaining not only their original arrangements of *cabinets-de-toilettes* leading off almost every bedroom, but their original furniture too – *bergères,* wash-stands, beds set in alcoves, and a large number of identical chests-of-drawers which were presumably ordered dozens at a time, and as a set must now be almost unique in France. The whole complex – the word is apt only because of the number and diversity of partition walls on this floor – shows exactly how a large household slept two hundred years ago. The master's bedroom and his companion's were downstairs ; the guests' above ; the servants above that. There was respect for privacy ; a surprising degree of concession to cleanliness of person

ABOVE *The dining-room at Montgeoffroy, in which the furniture is mainly Louis XV. The chair-seats are abnormally wide in proportion to the backs. The stove is also unusual, its flue disguised as a palm-tree in faience.* OPPOSITE *The backgammon table in the petit-salon at Montgeoffroy is one of the many articles that survive in their original positions from the furnishing of the late 18th-century house.* BELOW *One of the lovely upstairs bedrooms. Most of the beds, however, were not free-standing with canopies, but were placed in wall-niches after the normal French 18th-century fashion.*

2 Canapés de petit point

8 fauteuils a la Reine semblable

4 fauteuils quarrés de point
Hongrie

14 housses de toile à carreau
vert et blanc pour lesdits

4 Bergeres

4 fauteuils en }
cabriolets   osiclour.

8 chaises idem }

ABOVE *The Grand Salon, and* (ABOVE, RIGHT) *part of the inventory for furnishing the room in 1775, contemporary with the building of the house. Many of the pieces can still be identified, including the four Louis XVI bergères in velvet. The hanging lantern, and the candelabra on the chimneypiece, all of gilded bronze, are also original to the room.* OPPOSITE *The front of the house seen from the meadows on its approach. There are radiating avenues which form a perspective to the house, but like most great French châteaux, and unlike their English counterparts, there was no attempt to conceal Montgeoffroy from the public road.*

and tidiness of possessions; and great comfort, for these well-proportioned rooms are quiet and cosy. It must have been agreeable to lie abed in those alcoves, so beautifully patterned in *toiles de Jouy* or painted paper, and then to rise in the morning and swing back the heavy shutters on the view.

Even the kitchen and saddle room preserve much of the atmosphere of the late 18th century, without conscious antiquarianism. There are no horses left at Montgeoffroy, but there are still good cooks. The sadness of the Maréchal's later life has not been transmitted to these rooms. It is not the house of an old man who looked back with bitterness on the past and with fear to the future. It is the house of someone who believed that there was still much enjoyment to be gained from books, good company and fine furniture and pictures, and that these things would be enjoyed by his descendants. They are, but not only as the Maréchal foresaw. It is the family's house, but those branching avenues are now invitations for all to enter. The château is open to the public, and if the distant view of it is severe, closer acquaintance reveals its intimacy and charm.

Ickworth *Suffolk England 1792-1830*

Ickworth is remarkable for many things : its size, its date, the personality of its builder, the pertinacity of his descendants, and the treasures which it contains. It has been called a 'sublime folly', but a folly is a plaything, an architectural frolic, light-hearted in intention and usually uninhabitable. Ickworth, on the contrary, is an edifice of vast size (over six hundred feet from end to end and a hundred feet to the top of the dome) and a serious attempt to give a new shape to a traditional design. A large part of it has been lived in for nearly a century and a half.

But it is certainly eccentric, and for the date of its completion, 1830, an architectural anachronism, since by then the Palladian idea of two outlying classical buildings joined to a centrepiece by curving wings had been discarded in favour of smaller Regency houses, bow-fronted and compact. Look at the photograph of Ickworth from the air, the only direction from which it can be seen as a whole, for trees and shrubs conceal its great extent from ground level. Dominant in the centre stands the Rotunda, capped by a flattened dome and fronted by a portico comparable in size to that of the Pantheon in Rome. In itself the Rotunda is a splendid piece of architecture. A circular shape is always arresting, and in the whole of Britain there is no other private building where it has been employed on such a scale. In other domed houses like Castle Howard and Mereworth the dome rises from the middle of a rectangular base. At Ickworth the whole structure is curved, like a drum mounted on a tambourine, with a thick band of stuccoed brick sandwiched between them. Two heroic friezes ring the entire perimeter, and a balustrade forms a little coronet on top of the dome. These break the outline horizontally and impart animation to the whole. But vertically, too, the

architect has relieved the rotundity by employing lines of engaged columns, Ionic below, Corinthian above, which march like a stage-army of Grenadiers round the façade, the three tiers of windows between each pair transforming a temple into a house. It is very simple, yet exceedingly novel ; monumental, but not austere ; huge, but not overpowering ; classical, but geometrically daring. It has something of the majesty of the three-tiered papal tiara.

From the Rotunda spring the curving galleries. Each swells at the centre, as if it had swallowed something, into a rectangular room, which from outside prepares the eye for the transition from the Rotunda to the straight lines of the wings. The junction of the galleries with these wings is managed ingeniously by running them into antechambers, so that the wings stand unencumbered, decent but not spectacular examples of the late-Palladian country-house style.

OPPOSITE *Looking from the top of the dome towards the private wing of Ickworth. The attic storey was added by the 4th Marquess of Bristol after his accession in 1907. In the foreground is part of the curving corridor, which was widened at its centre to admit a square smoking-room.* BELOW *The Rotunda seen from the garden side, with the orangery (left) and the reverse side of one of the linking galleries. The Rotunda was intended by the 4th Earl of Bristol (the 'Earl-Bishop') as his main house, and the two wings for the display of his art collection. Only the Rotunda was completed externally at his death in 1803, but he never revisited Ickworth in time to see it.*

TOP *Ballyscullion in Ireland, the prototype of Ickworth, which the Earl-Bishop began to build in 1787, inspired by his sight of Belle Isle, a similar building on Lake Windermere. Ballyscullion was finished externally in 1793, when the Bishop was already busy with his plans for its greater successor, Ickworth. But he never lived in either house, and after his death Ballyscullion was levelled to the ground by his heir.*
ABOVE *Frederick Hervey, Bishop of Derry and 4th Earl of Bristol (1730-1803), the builder of Ickworth. This portrait by Vigée-Lebrun has Vesuvius in the background as a tribute to the Earl-Bishop's interest in vulcanology.*

The builder of Ickworth, Frederick Augustus Hervey, Bishop of Derry in Ireland and fourth Earl of Bristol, did not live to see one stone of his gigantic conception laid upon another. At the time of his death in 1803, the Rotunda had been completed as far as the roof, and the wings had risen a few feet above the ground. But after choosing the site and supervising the plans in 1792, the Earl-Bishop never returned there. He resumed his Continental travels, secure in the affections of his Irish flock, to whom his energy, wealth and political courage had brought great benefits in spite of prolonged absences from his See. He was an uncommon man. Vain and self-indulgent though he was, there was a magnificence about his enterprises that commanded the respect of humbler and less original people. He had never expected to succeed to the Bristol title or estates, being the youngest of three brothers, and was content with the Bishopric of Derry, one of the richest in the gift of the Crown, and with the leisure that it gave him to indulge his passions for travel, architecture and the collection of works of art. He built for himself in Ireland two great houses, Downhill in Antrim and Ballyscullion on the shores of Lough Beg. The latter was the prototype of Ickworth. It was not quite so large (the drum was 84 feet at its widest compared to Ickworth's 120) and the galleries terminated in a muddle of outhouses instead of classical wings. In other respects it was almost identical – an elliptical Rotunda, a four-columned portico, three storeys, a flattened dome and curving exterior corridors. The architect was Michael Shanahan of Cork. The house was never fully completed and the Bishop never lived there. It was levelled to the ground by the heir to his Irish estates in 1813.

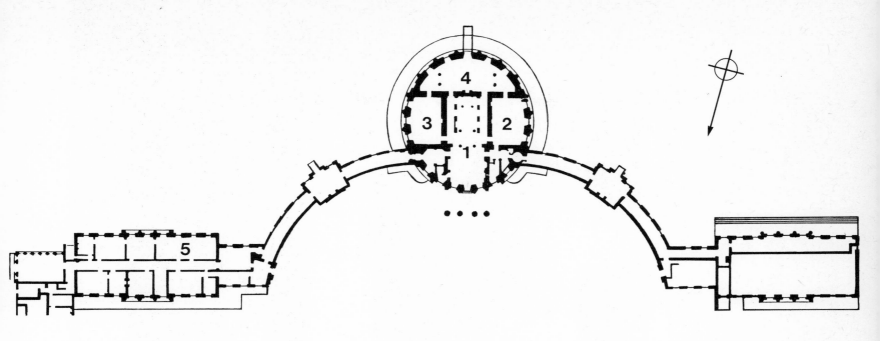

Both the Bishop's brothers predeceased him, and he succeeded to the Earldom and an additional £20,000 a year in 1779. The Herveys had lived in this part of East Anglia since the 15th century, first near the church, but later in a house, modest in comparison with the distinction of the family, which still stands, though much transformed, half a mile from its huge successor. The Earl-Bishop saw his opportunity to recreate Ballyscullion in a Suffolk park. He employed as his architect Francis Sandys, who was assisted by his brother, Joseph.

His purpose was to erect a palace for his own occupation during the infrequent occasions when he expected to be in England, and an art-gallery for the treasures which he had collected on the Continent. The Rotunda was to be his house : the wings, and the corridors connecting them, his art-gallery. This strange decision obliged him to create within an egg habitable rooms on three storeys, and to contrive in the centre some stately approach from the hall to the upper floors. How this puzzle was solved is among the most fascinating features of Ickworth. The problem was slightly eased by making the Rotunda elliptical instead of round, flattening the arc on each of the longer sides where the dining and drawing rooms lay, and so lessening the curvature of their outer walls. But at the bottom of the egg, which contained the library, the curve was correspondingly sharper, and internal columns were introduced at each end to disguise it. These three rooms, with the hall and staircase-well, occupy the whole of the ground floor and are thirty feet high. The curvature is not displeasing. It gives the effect of enormous bow windows, and only at the ceiling-level of the library is its awkwardness manifest.

TOP *The ground-plan of Ickworth makes clear that the Rotunda is not a perfect circle, as it appears from outside, but an oval. The state rooms are 1. Hall. 2. Dining-room. 3. Drawing-room. 4. Library. The Yellow Drawing-room in the private wing of the house is numbered 5.* ABOVE *The architect's original wooden model is still in the house. Here is the Rotunda with its upper part removed, showing the arrangement of its ground-floor rooms. The U-shaped staircase was never built as planned.*

ABOVE *The dining-room in Ickworth's Rotunda contains the portraits of all the Hervey family who have used the room since its completion in about 1830. The Earl-Bishop's bust by J. Wilton is on the chimney-piece. The splendid collection of silver, some of which is seen on the table, was principally formed by 1st and 2nd Earls of Bristol in the 18th century.* OPPOSITE *The hall and staircase in the Rotunda were reconstructed after 1907. Four scagliola columns support the first floor, and at the back, under the dome, stands a great marble group by Flaxman, 'The Fury of Athamas', commissioned by the Earl-Bishop in Rome in 1790.*

Upstairs, where the rooms are smaller, it is scarcely apparent until you try to hang a picture against an exterior wall. Connecting the storeys, there was to have been a U-shaped staircase, visible in the original wooden model of the house, but this was never built as designed, and the temporary staircase was replaced early in the present century by a square stairway from which, at different levels, you can look down upon the hall below. The dome, internally, is lost. Part of it can be glimpsed through a skylight, but the glorious effects of other domed halls are not reproduced here.

The corridors to the two wings are wide and high enough to form more than mere passageways. They are galleries in their own right, with vaulted ceilings, bookcases fitted to the curve, and floors of narrow planks curved by a masterpiece of carpentry to follow the line of the walls. The west gallery leads to a wing which was never finished internally and now holds an orangery running the whole length of the southern side, and a large

store-room now containing a grain-dryer, in place of the sculpture for which it had been intended. The east gallery leads to the family's own wing, closed to the public but holding in reserve for the privileged visitor the supreme pleasure of this house.

When the Bishop died in 1803, his second son and heir, Frederick William, fifth Earl and first Marquess of Bristol, waited for more than twenty years before completing the house. It is astonishing that he ever did so, for the design and scale of it were already outmoded, and the Bishop's art-collection was confiscated when the French entered Rome in 1798, and subsequently dispersed. The expense must have been enormous. Nevertheless, the first Marquess honoured his father's undertaking, but reversed his intention to inhabit the Rotunda and devote the two wings to display. The Rotunda was indeed finished more or less as the Bishop had planned, and it was used on grand occasions, but a self-contained house was fashioned within the east wing by introducing a second floor. Later a top storey was added by the fourth Marquess.

This is the house which the present, sixth, Marquess now inhabits. In a short space it is difficult to do justice to the controlled magnificence of these rooms. The Bishop's dream has been fulfilled, though not as he expected it, for his 'art-gallery' is no mere exhibition space, but a finely finished house in which works of art form the background to a family's daily life. The appearance, but not the structure, of these rooms has been transformed by renovations which the Marquess and his wife began soon after his succession in 1960. The house is filled with light, by day from great windows facing the garden, by night from Venetian chandeliers hanging along the corridors which bisect it from end to

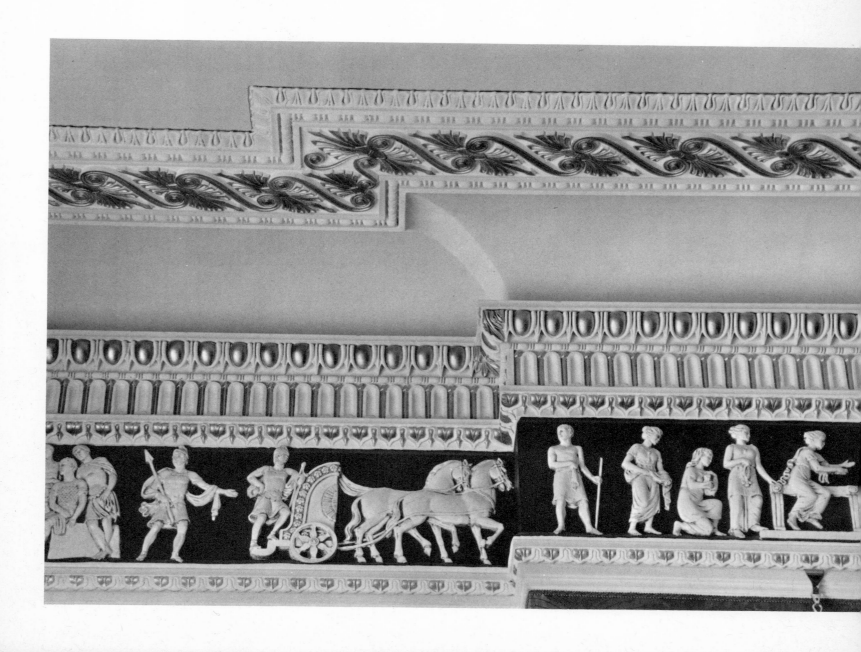

RIGHT *The upper corridor of the east wing, now occupied by the 6th Marquess of Bristol. The gallery on
the right with its Ionic columns and ironwork rails
was inserted as part of the redecorations in the 1960s.
The chandeliers are some of those commissioned by the
present Marquess in Venice.* BELOW *During the redecoration of the dining-room in the east wing, the
classical frieze on the outside of the Rotunda was in
part copied for this dominant position round the walls.*

end along both main floors. It is these corridors which unify the house, giving access to rooms opening on each side, and broad enough to be filled with works of art which stand away from the walls or hang against them, and so break up their great length by a constant change of colour, shape, texture and lighting. Variety is further added by ingenious changes of internal level. A mezzanine is entered from halfway up the staircase, and to allow room for it, the bedroom floor on the entrance side is raised another quarter-storey, leading off a gallery which runs alongside, and five steps above, the upper corridor. A house of moderate, but not modest, size is thereby made to appear much larger than it really is, and infinitely more comfortable and pleasing than the high rooms and difficult ascents of the Rotunda which the Earl-Bishop thought necessary for his status and his health.

The main room downstairs is the Yellow Drawing-room, named after its silk wall-coverings, and in this description it must be allowed to represent the others. Until recently it was two rooms, formed into one by replacing a dividing wall by an Ionic column on each side. The doors are of tooled mahogany, with white and gilt door-frames brought from the Bristols' house in St James's Square, London. The four windows are curtained like miniature prosceniums. The carpets, based on an Aubusson design, were commissioned in Kashmir. The marble chimneypiece at the west end is by Canova, one of the few pieces from the Earl-Bishop's collection to have reached England. On the walls hang works by Velasquez, Guercino, De Ribera, Kneller and Van Dyck. But it is the furniture which makes the most lasting impression. Much of it, both English and French, has been collected by the present Marquess, and all of it, as throughout the house, is in perfect, gleaming condition. Little 18th-century side-tables poised tiptoe on the parquet floor, a Hepplewhite work-table with an ormolu gallery, two Louis XV writing-tables and a suite of Louis XVI chairs and sofa – all these share in this room the best traditions of three centuries. Almost every colour is found on or between the walls – black and gilt and white and mahogany and yellow, the red in the pictures, the pale blue of the frieze, the darker yellow of the carpets – and the whole room is so carefully balanced both in its colour scheme and in the choice and placing of the objects, that its considerable length is disguised, and a connoisseur's dream becomes a pleasant sitting-room where one feels unconstrained by the fear of knocking anything over.

The two phases of Ickworth, the Earl's and the Marquess's, now lead separate existences. The Rotunda, a miraculous compromise with eccentricity, which houses an art-collection almost equally fine and well displayed, is on view to the public, and the contents belong to the National Trust. The east wing might be five miles, instead of four hundred feet, away. Its appearance, its approach, its use, its whole character, are utterly different, and all the contents are Lord Bristol's. But together they form an architectural unity which is too splendid to be ridiculed for its extravagance, and in both much of the taste and boldness of the Earl-Bishop has been enshrined.

OPPOSITE *The Yellow Drawing-room is the main room in the private wing of Ickworth, and was converted by the 6th Marquess in the 1960s. Two rooms were formed into one by knocking out a dividing wall and substituting the Ionic columns.* ABOVE *The silk wall-coverings were manufactured to an Adam design based on those in the Green-silk Drawing-room at Buckingham Palace. The chimneypiece was made for the Earl-Bishop by Canova.*

Beauregard House *New Orleans USA 1825-6*

Walking through the old French quarter of New Orleans, you will pass many houses of which the dominant features are strange iron balconies (*galeries* to the French, *miradors* to the Spaniards) which sometimes extend round the corners of the buildings and reach down to street level. These balconies are the sure mark of a New Orleans house. If it were not for their tiered and lacey elegance, the *vieux Carré* might be thought shoddy and rather uninteresting. The British colonial style in equivalent planters' towns like Charleston, with its Georgian fronts and gay porticoes, is neater and outwardly much more attractive. But what we see today in New Orleans is not the French colonial city. Only a single building, the Ursuline convent facing Beauregard House, survives from the period of French rule. We see the city of the Creoles, that amalgamation of the French, Spanish and West Indian aristocracy who rebuilt New Orleans following the disastrous fires of 1788 and 1794. We owe these modest townhouses with their immodest balconies to them, and to several generations of American immigrants who flooded into Louisiana after its purchase by the United States in 1803. A distinctive style had been established by the Creoles. It was followed for another fifty or sixty years. The balconies grew in number and competitive complexity against the earlier façades, and they impart to New Orleans a character which seems more ancient and more European than it really is.

Towards the end of one of the main streets you will suddenly come upon a brick house of very different appearance. Beauregard House is the product of careful architecture compared to the brick and iron jumble of its neighbours, and its style is unparalleled in the rest of the city. It was built in 1825-6 for an auctioneer and slave-dealer, Joseph Le Carpentier, by an architect called François Correjolles. It is usually assumed from his surname that he was a Spaniard. In fact, like his client, he was more probably French in upbringing. His family, originating from San Domingo in the West Indies, emigrated to Baltimore at the end of the 18th century, and thence to New Orleans, where François first came

ABOVE *Beauregard House in 1866. Its architecture is known as the raised-cottage style, which confined the bedrooms and living-rooms to the first floor, under which a service corridor led at street-level to the courtyard behind. Carriages turned in by the gates on the left.* OPPOSITE *The rear of the house, with a long porch on the first floor and, below, the corridor leading to the lower of the two street-doors.* BELOW *The ironwork at the front of the house replaced earlier wooden railings in about 1840. The designs were Spanish in origin, but the great majority of New Orleans iron balconies were of American manufacture, though it was only in this city that they achieved such prominence.*

to live as a boy and where he practised architecture for the remainder of his life. He is not known to have designed any building before Beauregard, and if this was his first attempt, it was also his most remarkable.

The house broke with tradition in several ways. The most obvious was to place at the entrance-front an elaborate four-columned portico approached from the street by a curving flight of steps at either end and surmounted by a large pediment. In 1825 this was a normal device of Federal architecture, but it had never been seen in New Orleans before. That the balustrades were originally of wood, replaced by iron in the 1840s, is another indication of the architect's refusal to be influenced by local fashion. Within the house his innovations were even more startling. From a long wide hall running the full depth of the house, doors opened to three bedrooms on the left and a saloon and dining room on the right. Beyond there was a reentrant porch with *cabinets* on each side. These rooms comprised the main floor of the house, for below there was nothing but a basement podium, and above, some garrets lit by dormers. The traditional New Orleans house was constructed on quite different principles. The entrance was not at the front, but at the rear, to which access was given by a tunnel from the street large enough for coach and horses to pass through to the courtyard behind. From this courtyard there was normally an interior staircase leading to the main floor, on which all the rooms would lead one into the next without corridor or hall. The greater convenience of Correjolles's arrangement is very obvious. What is surprising is that with the influx of north-eastern Americans into New Orleans, it was not widely imitated.

However, Correjolles (or his client) insisted on retaining some of the features of the 'French' houses that have made New Orleans so individual a city. The main floor was raised well above ground-level to catch the river-breezes, and behind was the usual courtyard or patio, round which were ranged quarters for the slaves. Furthermore, a service tunnel, for people on foot only, penetrated the basement from back to front, approached by the door under the portico and leading to the patio behind. Inside, too, one can see the Creole influence in the high rectangular rooms with elliptical fanlights above each door. A wide opening between the saloon and dining-room was probably made some twenty years after the house was built, and the flanking Ionic pilasters added at the same date. But basically the house has not been changed externally or internally since 1826.

The architectural importance of Beauregard is therefore its combination of Creole tradition with American innovation. The house is the product of the fairly rapid changes in Louisiana's political status – French for over sixty years, Spanish for forty, American thereafter. Yet its charm lies not in the clever mingling of styles, but in its simplicity. One expects from the grandiose entrance a grand interior. One foresees an attempt to achieve dignity by the piling-on of Georgian or classical ornament. But it does not give that effect at all. The long hallway is white, well-lit and bare. Its excellent proportions are enhanced by the opening

of many double doors throughout its length, each surmounted by a fanlight. The bedrooms are large and cool, the reception rooms capacious more than splendid. There is little decoration. The fireplaces are of plainly cut marble imported from New York, and at ceiling level there are plaster cornices and central roses to support the chandeliers, quite elaborate by current New Orleans standards. Otherwise the house receives its character from its furniture. It is a framework for people, for their possessions, activities and friends. It was not designed for arrogant display, and it does not contain any.

The surprise of the house is at its far side. The hall ends in a small dining room which overlooks the patio across a verandah (probably added at a later date), and you descend by wooden steps to the paved centre of the court. It is shaded by a large oak-tree with a fountain in the middle, and on the three sides away from the house are the low buildings in some of which the slaves formerly lived and worked. It affords equal delight to the senses of sight, sound and smell. The little rooms have been converted into study, library, offices and two bedrooms. Their doors open either into each other or directly on to the patio. The walls are rosy bare brick or plastered, hung with tapestry, lined with books, or set with majolica in the arches of the old coach-house. The ceilings are formed by slender whitewashed rafters lying on a slight slope. Against the main house stir the shadows of the trees. The fountain tinkles. Little Negro boys run in and out unabashed. One feels that this secluded spot, for all its origins in slavery, has been the centre of much human affection.

Beauregard House has been known by that name for the last thirty years, and then because it was rescued from demolition by a group of people who were determined to preserve it in memory of the Confederate General P. G. T. Beauregard, the victor of the Battle of Bull Run, who took lodgings in the house for some eighteen months after the end of the Civil War. A few pieces of his furniture have been restored to the rooms. It is also sometimes claimed as the birthplace of Paul Morphy, the great American chess-master, whose grandfather was the Le Carpentier who built it. But this cannot be so, according to Samuel Wilson Jr., the leading architectural historian of New Orleans, since the City Register shows unmistakably that Le Carpentier sold the house some ten years before Paul was born. Its later history was one of mounting disaster. For a time it was a hideout for Italian immigrants who formed their own Mafia in New Orleans, murdering, among others, the Chief of Police. It then became a home for indigent layabouts. After the Society had moved in to save it from destruction, Mrs Frances Parkinson Keyes, the American author, took a lease of it in 1944, and restored first the slave-quarters and then by degrees the remainder of the house. She still spends part of the year there, and has passed the titular ownership to the Keyes Foundation. To her we owe not only two major novels, *Madame Castel's Lodger* and *The Chess Players*, which deal with different incidents in the history of the house, but its present atmosphere of calm after storm. Without her public spirit and determination, the house might not even be standing today.

ABOVE *Over the door to one of the living-rooms at Beauregard is this typical fanlight of the 1825 period.* BELOW *The courtyard at the back of the house is surrounded by buildings on all four sides, of which the rear building, seen here, was originally the slave-quarters, converted by Mrs Frances Parkinson Keyes into bedrooms and sitting-rooms. One of the side-rooms is seen* OPPOSITE. *Part of her collection of fans and majolica is displayed in the brick arch of the old coach-house, with an iron staircase leading from it.*

Lyndhurst *Tarrytown New York USA 1832-67*

One of the pleasing paradoxes of America's architectural history is that private houses were built on so modest a scale compared to the ambition of their owners and the immensity of the landscape. Lyndhurst is a good example of this. It stands on a bluff over-looking the Hudson River some twenty miles north of New York. The Hudson is huge, more like an arm of the sea than a river, and you would require field-glasses to count the number of windows in houses on the opposite shore. Its builder was a General William Paulding, a former Congressman and Mayor of New York at the time of La Fayette's visit in 1825. He built expensively in marble quarried by the prisoners of neighbouring Sing Sing, and the elaboration of the interior indicates a purse that was certainly deep. But by contemporary European and later American standards it was an unassuming house. It contained no more than a hall, two reception rooms, a dining room, an office, a library and six or seven bedrooms, some very small. Yet this was the house which Philip Hone, Paulding's political rival, could des-cribe, with consternation more than malice, as 'a magnificent house . . . An immense edifice resembling a baronial castle, or rather a Gothic monastry. If I mistake not, it will one of these days be designated as Paulding's Folly.' It was named, more conventionally, 'Knoll'.

Hone's ridicule was directed more at the style than at its extravagance. Lyndhurst (the name was altered with the change of owner in 1864) was one of the earliest Gothic Revival houses to

The original house on the Hudson built for William Paulding in 1832-42 is shown ABOVE *in Davis's own drawing for his client. The same front as it is today is shown* OPPOSITE. *Several features of the first house can still be identified, including the crocket-ted gable and the smaller of the two towers on the right. The heavy porte-cochère and the taller tower were added by Davis in 1864-67 when the house was doubled in size for George Merritt.*

301

be built in America, one of the very best of its kind, and one of the few to have survived intact. To contemporaries it must have appeared extraordinary. For some time Americans had been building publicly and privately in the 'pure' Greek and Roman style. It no longer struck them as strange to set down a complete Roman temple in a city centre, like Jefferson's Capitol at Richmond, Virginia, nor to reproduce the lines of the Erechtheum from Maine to Georgia. But for a respectable citizen like Paulding to borrow the Gothic style was a bold innovation. He was seventy at the time, and he owned a decent 18th-century house in the same district of Tarrytown. He was persuaded by his son Philip and by his architect, Alexander J. Davis, to experiment in a manner that Davis's firm had already tried out at Glen Ellen, near Baltimore, the first of their large Gothic Revival houses actually to be erected. Lyndhurst was the second.

Davis was the master of a whole repertory of other styles at a time when an indigenous American architecture had yet to be evolved. In his diary he later made a note of what he was able to offer his clients :

> 'American log-cabin, Frame House, English cottage, Collegiate Gothic, Manor house, French suburban, Switz cottage, Lombard Italian, Tuscan from Pliny's villa in Ostia, Ancient Etruscan, Suburban Greek, Oriental, and Castellated.'

You could take your pick. Of all these, the Collegiate Gothic which Davis recommended for Lyndhurst was the strangest importation. For while the others might with ingenuity be adapted to the requirements of a country house by modifying their lines out of all recognition (his 'Oriental', for example, was really Regency), the Gothic was the least domesticated style of all. It was ecclesiastical, pointed and severe. Though romantic, it was ill-suited to the American generosity of character and landscape. It was cold and dark within. If Gothic were to be chosen at all, the Tudor yeoman style would have been preferable to the monastic. For a house, the scale of Gothic architecture was wrong. It was designed to soar, not crouch. It was spiritual in its associations, not homely. Nor had it any but the most indirect link with the thrusting America of the early 19th century. The heraldic shields on the fireplaces and vaulted ceilings of Lyndhurst are left significantly blank.

But Davis was imitating an imitation. He drew his inspiration from the English Gothic Revival which Horace Walpole had introduced eighty years before, and which was then being immensely elaborated by Pugin, who began with Barry to build the new Houses of Parliament in the same year as Lyndhurst was commissioned. Davis persuaded himself that 'the English Collegiate style is to be preferred to Greek for country houses . . . It admits of greater variety both of plan and outline, while its big windows, oriels, turrets and chimney shafts give a pictorial effect'. He knew of Strawberry Hill, and had access to the published drawings of the Pugins and Britton and many other works of the English Gothic revivalists. But he had never been to Europe, and never in his life saw an original Gothic building.

ABOVE *A drawing made by Davis in 1865 during the enlargement of Lyndhurst. It shows the oriel window of the great tower.* BELOW *is one of Davis's windows as executed. He had mastered antique models without slavishly imitating them, although he never saw an original Gothic building in his life.* OPPOSITE *Lyndhurst from its approach side, revealing a glimpse of the Hudson beyond on the left, just south of the Tappan Zee bridge.*

A watercolour drawing of the completed Lyndhurst from the river side. In the second period of building, 1864-67, Davis added to his original house the tall tower and everything to the left of it. 'Graceful, finely proportioned and intricately balanced, it is a masterpiece of asymmetrical composition', wrote Jane B. Davies in her description of the house.

Nevertheless, Lyndhurst was externally a great success. It was built in two stages. The original house, erected for Paulding in 1832-42, was doubled in size by Davis twenty-five years later for the second owner, George Merritt, a New York merchant, by adding the tall tower, an extra set of rooms to the north, a *porte-cochère* on the entrance front and another storey over part of the Paulding house. In this description the two periods will be treated as one, since the architect was the same, the style the same, the material the same, and the two halves of the house are so indistinguishable that the first seems incomplete without the second, almost as if Davis had had the full design in mind from the very start, and had only been waiting for the advent of an even wealthier and more ambitious patron to complete it. In the interval, his assurance had increased. He built higher and stronger. His Gothic features became more adventurous, and if in the decoration of some of the later rooms he at last overreached himself, it was with a flourish. The 'new' parts of Lyndhurst marked the end of the picturesque phase of America's Gothic Revival just as the 'old' parts marked its beginning.

The house is approached through the fine ornamental trees of Merritt's park. The silhouette is composed of towers, gables, and crocketted pinnacles, asymmetrically disposed, as if to suggest growth over centuries instead of over years, with two main features rising above the rest, a tall belfry-like tower and an apparent chapel, separated and extended by short ranges, more Tudor than Gothic, more 'collegiate' than ecclesiastical. The pale walls are frequently and variously broken, once by a huge Gothic window with elaborate tracery, once by an oriel, once by a high Tudor double bay, and many times by transomed windows with labels above them. The result is not fussy. There is no

quaintness about it. The temptation to which later Victorians succumbed, to throw at a Gothic façade every motif in the architectural textbooks, was here resisted. The longer one looks at the outside of Lyndhurst, the better its proportions appear. For example, move the tower in imagination a few feet to the right or left, heighten or lower it by an extra storey, and it will immediately seem ungainly. The *porte-cochère*, a Merritt addition, looks rather too heavy because it is baronial and castellated, instead of elegant and trim, but externally it is the only error. Notice how Davis contrived to introduce a wide porch – he called it a 'piazza' or 'umbrage' – round two sides of the original house without disturbing the balance or making nonsense of his chosen period. The piazza softens the rigidity of the house, reaches out from it towards the surrounding park, and forms a series of canopied stages where it must have been pleasant to sit on a summer's evening looking at the huge river below. Skimpy trees growing close to the house have now obscured the river-view.

The outside of Lyndhurst has nobility because its constituent parts are noble in origin and associations and they are grouped together convincingly. But carry the same theme indoors and it becomes questionable. The rooms lose much in convenience from their Gothic strait-jacket, and gain little from it in dignity. They strain after mediaeval effects which the middle ages never imagined. It is difficult to know quite what Davis intended. His motive was certainly not playful, like Horace Walpole's 'small capricious house' on the Thames, for the rooms are in their strange way solidly respectable. Nor was it antiquarian, since he allowed himself deviations from the Gothic in his parquet floors, plaster painted to look like marble, smooth-sliding doors, flat ceilings alternating with the vaulted, and copies of angelic

TOP *The large window of the art-gallery was altered by the Goulds, as can be seen by comparing it with the same feature in the watercolour opposite. The number of mullions was reduced, and clear glass substituted for stained glass, making its appearance slightly less ecclesiastical.* ABOVE *Part of the 'piazza' which dates from the earlier period of the house, and provided elegant verandahs from which to enjoy the river view.*

figures by Raphael painted between the joists. Perhaps it was romantic, in the sense that A. J. Downing, the landscapist and Davis' close collaborator, intended when he wrote, 'Rural Gothic is best suited to our northern broken country,' as if the Hudson were the Rhine. But there remains an impression of aimlessness about the interior of Lyndhurst, which contrasts strongly with the certainty of Davis' touch on the outside.

The outer hall, the original *porte-cochère* glassed in, is excellent because it is not in the least mediaeval. It is cool and light and unselfconscious. So too are the drawing-room (more like a pavilion than a monastic chamber), and the Merritt end of the library which is intimate and interestingly shaped. But the disasters of the house, though interesting examples of Victorian decoration and considerably altered at later dates, are the two rooms

OPPOSITE *The library contains at least one example of the Gothic furniture which Davis designed for the house, and which has descended through three families and several generations. The book collection is that of Jay Gould.* BELOW *The drawing-room at Lyndhurst was redecorated and refurnished in the 1880s by the Goulds in the style of Beaux Arts classicism. The other main rooms were left much as the Pauldings and Merritts had known them.*

on which Davis expended his greatest care. The 'new' dining-room is ceilinged with *café-au-lait* beams as heavy and closely spaced as the deck-beams of a man-of-war, and so excessively ornamented that the room must have stifled the laughter of any children admitted to it. The gallery on the first floor has a baronial roof and a huge Gothic window which fail to produce an air of antiquity while rendering it uncomfortable and bleak. Sad to say, it is architecturally shoddy. It looks less like a gentleman's art-gallery than a village hall which might occasionally be hired for strictly proper purposes and a modest fee. The pictures are there to hide the walls.

Lyndhurst was sold in 1880 to Jay Gould, a railway tycoon who made a lot of money and enemies. He and his two daughters, who in turn succeeded him as proprietor, had the taste to understand that something so eccentric was a work of art. They added to the furnishings which Davis had designed in the Gothic style for the Pauldings and Merritts and which had always been sold with the house, and they installed electricity and more bathrooms. Otherwise they left the house untouched. When the second daughter, Anna Gould (who had become the Duchess of Talleyrand-Périgord), died in 1961, she left Lyndhurst to the National Trust for Historic Preservation. It contains today the legacies of the three families, Paulding, Merritt and Gould, superimposed within a single house. There is a slight overburden of heirlooms, rather too many stuffed chairs in the bedrooms, a really dreadful Cupid in the drawing room and some bad coloured glass. But the inside of Lyndhurst had been from the start an uncertain compromise. What matter are its exterior and the idea behind it – the idea that the Americans might use the English Gothic as an instrument to break open the classical mould in which their architecture had for so long been encased. If the idea itself was second-hand, its execution by Davis was a masterpiece, and Lyndhurst is now rightly regarded as among America's most important architectural documents from the past.

ABOVE *The dining-room in the 1860s part of Lynd-hurst. The furniture was probably designed for Mer-ritt by Davis. In contrast to the clean and reticent lines of the exterior, one feels in this room the impact of the exuberantly lush Victorian taste.* TOP LEFT *The large room on the first floor was originally designed by Davis as a library and music room. Before the altera-tion of the huge end-window, and when bookcases in-stead of pictures lined the walls, the room must have appeared less forbidding than it does today.* OPPO-SITE *The Pauldings' main bedroom served as a guest-room for the Goulds. It is now furnished in ac-cordance with the Gould inventory of 1894. The Gothic bedstead is similar to designs made for Mer-ritt by Davis.*

Schloss Herrenchiemsee *Bavaria Germany 1878-86*

The last house to be described in this book is the strangest; not at first sight, for it seems grand and conventional, but in its origins. It is an imitation of Versailles built on a lake-islet by King Ludwig of Bavaria. It is unfinished, since all work ceased when he was certified insane and the control of the privy purse was taken out of his hands. But the very considerable part which was completed, inside and out, was the achievement of only eight years, 1878-86. At the same time he was still building his vast romantic castle of Neuschwanstein, having added the finishing touches to his rococo castle of Linderhof, as well as planning in detail a gothic castle at Falkenstein and an Indian castle for the shores of the Plansee. His building mania was his undoing. It was cited as evidence of his insanity; it almost bankrupted his kingdom; it led to his abdication and early death. But it left behind buildings which have so entranced later generations that the State has recouped the original expenditure many times over from the revenue of tourism. How King Ludwig would have rounded on his enemies could he have known that eighty years after his death the German Tourist Board would select Neuschwanstein as the illustration for their main poster advertising the beauty and richness of the country! It has been seen all over the world and mistaken by many for a crowning achievement of the Middle Ages instead of a last romantic spasm of the late 19th century. Herrenchiemsee is no less remarkable, though less obviously dramatic; and it presents an even stranger problem in human psychology than its predecessor.

After a visit to Versailles in 1874, King Ludwig II returned to Bavaria full of ideas for erecting a near-replica of it on the island of Herrenchiemsee, which he had purchased the year before. The exterior of the palace was completed in little more than three years and then the decorations of the rooms began. His architect was C. von Dollmann, who was succeeded by J. von Hofmann in 1883. OPPOSITE *is the back of the house. Only the staterooms on the first floor were finished internally.*

The problem is this. Ludwig II was a romantic. His intimacy
with Wagner stimulated his sense of union with the world of the
Old German sagas. He liked waterfalls, jagged Alpine scenery,
half-ruined towers swimming in mist, and midnight winter drives
in ski-sledges drawn by six white horses. He hated society, was
disillusioned with politicians, and became so solitary a recluse
that he could not even tolerate the presence of a servant in his
dining-room, let alone a guest to share his meal or a wife his bed.
Neuschwanstein and Linderhof, and his other romantic projects
which were never executed, are therefore understandable. They
were built deep in mountains and reflected architecturally the
awefulness of the landscape and emotionally the dominant mood
of their creator. But Herrenchiemsee is something quite different.
Certainly its island site promises seclusion, but the mountains are
hidden by trees except from the roof of the house, and the style of
the whole building is in every respect the opposite of what Ludwig craved. It was un-German, it was un-gothic, it was un-
romantic, it glorified war, it demanded a thronging and servile
court, it was built for display, it needed a Queen as well as a King,
and it was a fake. The explanation of this extraordinary contradic-
tion lies in Ludwig's admiration for Louis XIV's achievement as a
monarch, and in his passion for architectural experiment. His
other castles had proved what he could do in his native idiom;
now he was attempting to translate the French 17th century into
the German 19th. At the same time it was a political gesture. It
was an expression of his contempt for politicians, a display of the
power which resided in him as King, but which he all too rarely
chose to exercise. His cousin and intimate, the Empress Elisabeth
of Austria, was fond of consoling him in his moments of depres-
sion with her own motto, 'But after all we can do whatever we
like!' Ludwig liked most to build, whatever the protests of his
Ministers, and at Herrenchiemsee the fact of the building and the
nature of the building were both assertions of his rights.

The garden as well as the house on Herrenchiemsee was closely modelled on Versailles by Ludwig II, King of Bavaria LEFT. The reclining goddess in the foreground is based very obviously on the river series of sculptures at Versailles, even to repeating the exact shape of the plinth. On the left is the Glory Fountain.

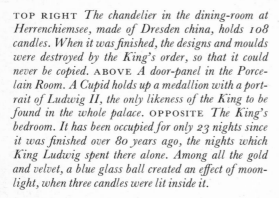

So we have a palace designed with its gardens to cover almost the whole of the flat island in the Chiemsee, like an airfield its atoll, and containing room after room decorated with overwhelming lavishness for a king who had only himself to satisfy. He spent no more than twenty-three nights here in all his life. He never entertained. The vast *salons* never saw a courtier, nor the gorgeously decked State bedroom a single occupant. It was only after his death that profane eyes looked upon all this gaudiness, and felt a bemused admiration for a man who could carry through so outrageous a concept. The melancholy of his life and death, the beauty of his person, the love which he inspired – all this in retrospect excuses many of Ludwig's follies. It does not wholly excuse Herrenchiemsee.

Versailles was more than an influence. The general arrangement of the rooms, including such famous features as the Hall of Mirrors, and much of the detail, has been followed very closely. Sometimes the copy is bigger and even more encrusted with ornament than the original. There are rooms at Herrenchiemsee which are repellent. Both bedrooms (there was no time to build more) arouse amazement more than admiration, and their perfect, unused, condition only emphasises the impossibility of sleeping in such a place. They have the unreal quality of waxworks. But there are other rooms where the ornament is less vivid, and where good workmanship in wood and glass and marble and ceramics has been allowed to speak without overemphasis. The best rooms are those like the Porcelain Room, where the artists have devised variants on the fashions of their

314

own day instead of copying the past, or the King's Guard Room, where the marble plaques are muted and the parquet flooring exquisite. The State staircase is not among the palace's most successful achievements, but at the opposite end is its pair, unfinished, left bare to its brick walls and wooden ceiling, a surviving example of the canvas on which Ludwig's army of artists worked. Standing there today one can recover something of the emotion which the King must have experienced in visualising the finished effect. The palace makes the impression which he intended – that the builder and owner of such a place was a man whose will could not be contradicted when he chose to state it, and a man in whom admiration for a style of living did not necessarily imply indulgence in all its vices. King Ludwig himself paid many visits to Versailles incognito, and sent his workers there to study and make drawings. But Herrenchiemsee is something more than a German imitation of what the French had conceived two centuries before. It is not a translation, but a restatement.

ABOVE *The King's Guard Room, which of all the magnificent rooms at Herrenchiemsee best expresses King Ludwig's hero-worship of Louis XIV. All the paintings are of the French King's wars (above the fireplace, the battle of Neerwinden), and the busts are of his favourite marshals – Condé, Turenne, Vauban and Villars. But the room is nevertheless one of the most subdued in the palace, and one of the most successful.* RIGHT *The Hall of Mirrors is even bigger and more splendid than its prototype at Versailles. It is nearly 100 yards long. It is decorated throughout in marble and gold-leaf, and the floor is inlaid with rosewood. Thirty-three crystal chandeliers and forty candelabra hold 2,188 candles, which are regularly lit for music recitals. There is still no electricity.*

The work on the embellishment of Herrenchiemsee was halted in 1886 by the King's enforced abdication and death in the same year. One staircase (OPPOSITE) was finished. Its pair (BELOW RIGHT) remains bare to its bricks and boards. Of the two flights of stairs in the finished hall, one led to the staterooms, the other to the uncompleted apartments of a nonexistent Queen. BELOW The curious mechanism by which the King's table in the dining-room could be wound down to the kitchen level and sent up again with fresh food, so that he would never be obliged to endure the presence of a servant in the room. When the table disappeared through the floor, two flaps sealed off the void automatically.

Is it proof of his insanity? Directly, no. As well might one charge England's Prince Regent with insanity for building the Pavilion at Brighton, which is far more eccentric than Herrenchiemsee. But it was a childish, irresponsible and unnecessary thing to do, and so extravagant that it is no surprise to find that the building costs accounted for a large share of the 21 million mark debt with which King Ludwig saddled his Treasury. Yet there is a fairy-tale quality about it, in the fact that the rooms which were finished are more royal than any royal rooms have ever been, even at Versailles. The acreage of gold-leaf applied, the number of candles required to light it (the palace still has no electric lighting), the purple bed-hangings which thirty women, it is said, spent seven years embroidering – all these details lusciously recounted to the tourists draw sighs of wonder in a dozen languages for the mingled splendour and tragedy of this young king's life. They reach their crescendo not in the Hall of Mirrors, gorgeous though that is, but in the dining-room, where a table set for four places could be cranked down below the floor and sent up again laden with the King's next course, so that he would not have to see or be seen by any menial. Four places? Yes, the other three were for his imaginary guests, the Marquise de Pompadour, Madame de Maintenon and Louis XIV, with whom the King could be heard conversing in low tones.